THE HEALING SPIRIT

THE HEALING SPIRIT

Embracing the Healing Spirit
Between and Within Us

Vincent L. Perri

Universal-Publishers
Irvine • Boca Raton

The Healing Spirit: Embracing the Healing Spirit Between and Within Us

Disclaimer
All the patients discussed in this book are composites of multiple cases so that their actual identity is concealed. Any similarity to any person in this book is purely coincidental. This book cites examples from the Judaic, Christian and Buddhist traditions but is not intended to acknowledge any one religious persuasion over another.

Universal Publishers, Inc.
Irvine, California • Boca Raton, Florida • USA
www.Universal-Publishers.com
2019

ISBN: 978-1-62734-272-8 (pbk.)
ISBN: 978-1-62734-273-5 (ebk.)

Typeset by Medlar Publishing Solutions Pvt Ltd, India

Cover design by Ivan Popov

Publisher's Cataloging-in-Publication Data
provided by Five Rainbows Cataloging Services

Names: Perri, Vincent L., 1953- author.
Title: The healing spirit : embracing the healing spirit between and within us / Vincent L. Perri.
Description: Irvine, CA : Universal Publishers, 2019. | Includes bibliographical references.
Identifiers: LCCN 2019934077 | ISBN 978-1-62734-272-8 (paperback) | ISBN 978-1-62734-273-5 (ebook)
Subjects: LCSH: Conversation--Psychological aspects. | Self-help techniques. | Psychology, Applied. | Jung, C. G. (Carl Gustav), 1875-1961. | Buber, Martin, 1878-1965. | Heschel, Abraham Joshua, 1907-1972. | BISAC: PSYCHOLOGY / Mental Health. | PSYCHOLOGY / Emotions.
Classification: LCC BF511 .P47 2019 (print) | LCC BF511 (ebook) | DDC 158.1--dc23.

DEDICATION

Jaime Perri
Your smile will always brighten the world.

David Perri
Loving the man that you've become.

TABLE OF CONTENTS

INTRODUCTION

There is something special about the space[1] between us when we meet. Something magical happens in this space when we encounter each other, and I hope to show how this seemingly ordinary space[2] is something extraordinary like an invisible matrix that connects us. I am convinced that in the space between you and I[3] there is something that invisibly connects us. Like a matrix between us it materializes like we are being connected by invisible dots that localize us in space and time. I have often marveled throughout my work as a doctor how the space between my patients and I always seemed to move and edge our interactions and dialogue in some uncharted direction. It seemed almost imperceptible at first, but the more I studied this invisible space the more I realized how real and tangible it was.

The space between two people is what I have called "the healing space."[4] It is a space that can be accessed and engaged when any one of two or more people encounter each other unconditionally.[5] Although we may not realize it, there are specific areas of our brain[6] that facilitate our movement into this healing space. These areas of our brain, however, must be nurtured to freely encounter the space in-between.[7] Deep in our brain there is a striatal complex[8] that coordinates our motor, memory, and cognitive functions[9] and unconsciously guides our movements, actions, and facilitation in space. These actions become a background pantomime[10] of unconsciously generated activity that swirls around us but provides a context of deeper archaic thought. It is this space between two people genuinely engaged in unconditional dialogue[11] that I believe opens a deeper "psychic space" within each of us that allows inner healing to occur. This, however, is not the end of the story.

Throughout recorded history mankind has always encountered what the renowned psychiatrist Carl Jung referred to as the numinous.[12] It is that deeply meaningful other worldly experience that occurs without any doubt of its spiritual or metaphysical origins.[13] It is the experience that occurs when you awaken from a dream and you marvel at what you know you experienced but are not exactly sure how it could have happened. It may have been an image, or an image associated with an emotional feeling, or maybe just a feeling that something beyond our ordinary experiences had taken place. These experiences are common to us all, and if we search far enough we will find that these experiences are replete in the biblical stories of old and all the mythologies and folklore of our ancestors. So, you may wonder, what does this have to do with the space between two people?

Any two people who have been engaged in serious, unconditional dialogue[14] will certainly affirm that there is a quality of the relationship that is far outside the bounds of ordinary social dialogue. Something unique happens in the space between them that allows them to engage each other in ways that intangibly transcend the boundaries of ordinary dialogue. Is it just the space "in-between,"[15] or is there something else that connects the dots along this invisible matrix?[16] Aren't these the same questions that are asked when anything supposedly magical happens between us? I believe that the "healing space"[17] is much more than just the space between two people. It is a special place where "relation"[18] takes on greater significance and allows greater participation of both the mind and the body.

It is this mind-body participation that occurs between two people in deep unconditional dialogue[19] that becomes the integrating factor that transcends the ordinary space between them. This space, which I believe can be transformed into a healing space, is not without psychological significance. The in-utero baby developing in the amniotic cavity almost appears to be symbiotically experimenting with space.[20] The baby moves about, grimaces, touches its face and ears, grins and smiles.[21] It begins to move its legs and arms[22] almost as if it's measuring space. In *space*, there is *symbiosis*.[23] This is a crucial underpinning to understanding the significance between two people when they meet in true unconditional dialogue.[24] This relationship between *space and symbiosis*[25] becomes the invisible network that links the two people in more than just conversation. When space and symbiosis[26] engage each other the world of *spirit*[27] is born, and I believe this is the bridge that allows unconditional dialogue[28] to occur. As I develop this concept I will also show that there is great historical significance in the presence of spirit from the Judeo-Christian tradition. I think there is much more to the Jewish philosopher Martin Buber's idea of "grace"[29] in the "I-Thou" relationship[30] than initially may meet the eye. This "grace"[31] may transcend our casual understanding of what we ordinarily think grace is.

Later I will examine a much deeper understanding of what I believe happens when two or more people engage each other unconditionally.[32] It is the "grace"[33] in Buber's "I-Thou"[34] that I believe is the pivotal element that emerges as a more transcendent function[35] of the two psyches joining in space. We will see how this symbiotic joining becomes the relation that brings space and symbiosis[36] to the emergence of spirit; what the eminent psychiatrist Carl Jung might call the transcendent function.[37] The transcendent function as we will see is not just a psychological process,[38] but will be shown as a concordant process along the lines of the Judeo-Christian tradition. In Jung's transcendent function[39] the unconscious and conscious psyche dynamically interact and evolve the process of individuation toward one's more individuated self. It is the process of relation,[40] but as it occurs within the psyche of the person. It is an intra-psychic relating removed from the dialogue of interpersonal relation as it might be construed in Buber's "I-Thou."[41] Although Buber was critical of the meditative practices and intra-psychic process when it removed the person from dialogue with some other,[42] it is also within the meditative practices and intra-psychic process that spirit may first be engendered.

Prayer is fundamentally an intra-psychic process of meditation. It is a dialogue of the most interpersonal nature with God or what the great Jewish philosopher Martin Buber would call "Thou."[43] By engaging prayer the person brings God or "Thou"[44] to a reality beyond his own psyche. Prayer in its meditative state becomes a process that expands the person's psychic space,[45] and opens the space "in-between"[46] to more meaningful dialogue. This is what I have referred to as the "Healing Space."[47] Historically we can examine Jesus in the Garden of Gethsemane.[48] The image engendered here is one of profound significance on many levels. If we consider this as an example of prayerful meditation it not only depicts the depth of solace and despair that can be expressed intra-psychically, but it goes further. Jesus returned to his apostles. He engaged them in dialogue. He created "space" between them.[49] He scolded them for not participating in his prayerful meditation.[50] It is this process of advancing and retreating from spirit to person in space that embodies only what human beings can do.

We can engender spirit in the space between us because we can engage spirit in the space within us. It is only possible to bring spirit to dialogue with some other if you first know what spirit is. To make a person a "Thou"[51] in Buber's meaning of the word we must first know God who is the ultimate "Thou."[52] We know God only through the means available to us as human beings.[53] God is unfathomable to our psyche except as images[54] or what Jung would refer to as the numinous.[55] It is only through our own inner search for God that we begin to glimpse the majesty of "Thou."[56]

This is the spirit in dialogue. Like all things both physical and metaphysical we must appreciate the interconnectedness[57] that embraces all of us and transcend the propensity to encapsulate every phenomenon into its own exclusive domain. I can become unconditionally present[58] for you because I first experience unconditionality[59] in the spirit.[60] This is how the meditative prayerful experience brings us to God or "Thou."[61] When I direct my thoughts to the quietude of prayer I seek dialogue within myself, but not with myself. I look to encounter the other which can only be God. It is this introversion within my own psychic space that becomes the spirit of relation. It is this inner dialogue that becomes the spirit of dialogue when I engage another. To those who think of prayer as a monologue without the other being present this idea may seem strange; however, true mindful meditation and prayer requires substantial listening to both the body and the soul. When Jesus prayed at Gethsemane[62] we must recognize that the silence in between His words was the soulful turning to God in dialogue.[63] Jesus then needed to substantiate His inner turning to God by entering the space of His apostles, and recreating His unconditional presence and dialogue[64] with them. This would have sealed "spirit and form"[65] and brought the more transcendent experience of His sorrow and prayer back to the human encounter. It is the human encounter that becomes the soul of the transcendent function.[66] This ultimately is what I believe Buber's emphasis on human dialogue comprises. It is not so much that meditation or its' prayerful counterpart is detrimental to human relation, but that it must be a servant to human relation in our evolution to unconditional presence in dialogue.[67]

We must never forget that "spirit and form"[68] is an ongoing evolution between any two or more people who meet in dialogue. I should make it clear that the depth of relation I discuss whenever any two or more people join each other in relation[69] deals more with the serious matters of life than the mundane, or what Buber would call the world of "It."[70] These are the moments when our unconditionality[71] can become a powerful force engaging the spirit of healing. It is the unconditional soulful attention to the grieving other that brings spirit to the space "in-between,"[72] and opens the psychic space[73] sufficiently to allow healing to occur. The psychic space is the inner domain of protective boundaries that we unconsciously develop from the time of our in-utero development to the present.[74] It is our inner psychic space that determines the unconscious boundaries of our outer spatial field, and how we will navigate this field with others. In this second book on this topic I hope to convey a deeper appreciation for the spiritual energies that are a part of every dialogue when at least one of the persons is unconditionally present.[75] In "The Healing Space"[76] my focus was on the *space* "in-between"[77] that became the unconscious battleground for the deeper archaic expression of pre-verbal speech. It is the space where our unconditional presence[78] for the other becomes the freedom for the other to unconsciously use space to metaphorically enact their deepest thoughts and emotions.

In *The Healing Spirit* the focus shifts from space to *spirit*. It is the spirit engendered in the unconditional presence[79] of the person or persons that connects them in space. The space "in-between"[80] is no longer simply an unconscious arena for the pantomime of meaningful movement, but it becomes a transformative space where "spirit and form"[81] come together. *Spirit* becomes the fundamental reality in the relationship. It is the invisible clandestine connection that links the unconditionality[82] of the person or persons in the process of dialogue. Spirit emerges as the "Thou" *in-between*.[83] It is this idea that Spirit, as it relates to Buber's "Thou,"[84] is not only within the person or persons but becomes the *presence*[85] between them. We find historical significance here in Christ's statement to His apostles in relation to the Holy Spirit or Comforter.[86]

Christ tells them that He is sending them a Comforter who will enter them and become an inner part of them.[87] Is this the seed of "Thou"?[88] His statement that He is with them always until the end of the age rings of the universal "Thou"[89] both within them and between them. Through unconditionality we are present for the other[90] and we engage the inner spirit or "Thou,"[91] but we also allow the inner spirit within us to universally emerge and unite us. In the Hebrew bible we read of the "spirit in man" as the "breath of the Almighty."[92] In relation to the Judaic tradition,

Buber addressed the unity of the Jews in relation to the indwelling God that became the unity within them.[93] In discussing this dualism within man, Buber addressed the unification of the soul through the unity of God within.[94]

This idea of the unification of opposites within the soul, or psyche, is closely aligned with Jung's reconciliation of opposites.[95] By reconciling our dualism we engage the transcendent function.[96] The transcendent function is the path that Jung elaborated in our inner approach to both individuate toward our higher self and integrate our dualities.[97] By engaging the transcendent function we reconcile our inner conflicts and complexes, and evolve to a more integrated being;[98] the God within can now emerge as the Spirit "in-between."[99] This is the essence of the healing spirit within us, and it is the essence of the healing spirit between us when we engage each other in unconditional dialogue.[100] It is interesting to note how Jung and Buber outwardly disagreed in their basic positions, and I often wonder if this wasn't simply because Jung's psychology crossed the boundaries between depth psychology and religion.[101] Contrarily, Buber's religious and Judaic explications often crossed the boundaries of depth psychology, and most likely led to a volatile attack on ego vulnerabilities. However, the unity that Buber discusses in relation to the indwelling "Thou" becoming unified in man, and in turn unifying God in man,[102] is a path that Jung's transcendent function in many ways aims to achieve.

The spirit in us is the sprit between us. It is the vibrational string[103] that is more than the space that separates us; it becomes the space that connects us. It is our unconditional presence for the other[104] that allows the spirit within to emerge as the spirit "in-between."[105] The unconditional presence that Buber elaborates in "I and Thou"[106] is a holy ground of compassionate silence. There is no greater gift that one can give to another than to offer the simple gesture of silence in listening.[107] Silence can become a powerful instrument in helping another heal from inner wounds that penetrate deeply. Our unconditional presence[108] becomes a focused intention of silent listening as we allow the other to express their deepest concerns. Our present age has evolved into a silentless cacophony that deafens the spirit within us and restrains the emergence of spirit between us. If we are to evolve our world we must evolve ourselves. Buber made this point clear in relation to the Judaic people becoming unified within themselves, so they could be unified as a people and community.[109]

Silence in dialogue is humility in listening. When we listen in soulful silence we express our undivided unconditionality[110] to the other. It is a way of expressing humility in the presence of the other's suffering. In silence, we invite the spirit within us to emerge and become the "grace"[111] that connects us. This is the miracle. This is the soul of all living creatures. It is the blood that gives life to the spirit and spirit to the person. We live in an ego-driven world that precludes the humility of the spirit. Jesus best described this humility on the Mount when He called the mourners meek and humble, and the merciful and persecuted the inheritors of the kingdom.[112] In some way, at some moment in time, we are all those others who mourn, are persecuted and made weak, or who suffer. This is the common thread of our connectedness. This thread is the road to the spirit. It is the path that we must travel if we are to make ourselves and the world better. Just think for one moment how the world would change if each of us simply humbled ourselves in the space we occupy.

This space is the holy ground. It is the space that connects us and becomes the space of the spirit between us. It is the chain of "grace"[113] that frees the hidden and repressed emotions that engender fear and reprisal. This may seem oversimplified and pretentious; however, it may be as simple as being responsible for our space. We no longer are a community-based people. Buber discussed this in relation to the Judaic people,[114] but now it is equally true of all of us. We have lost our ancestral heritage and no longer have ties to the soil of our ancestors. We live in a fast-tracked global society that has been watered down by a consumerism that thwarts the emergence of spirit. We no longer see the space between us because we have lost the soil under our feet. Our earth was once our common ground where life pulsed between us and became a part of the spirit within us. We have disrespectfully stripped our earth of its spirit and this has thwarted our inner spirit. We must reclaim our space because our space is a holy ground. The spirit within our soil is part of the spirit that pulses within our soul and becomes the life blood of our relationships.

Until we see the connection between our earth and ourselves and realize that the "grace"[115] of spirit is without bounds, we will never appreciate our life in the spirit of unconditionality.[116] When we further discuss the *spirit of embrace* we are going to explore these relationships in greater detail. It is no coincidence that Jung found his greatest solace working in the earth and developing his relationship with the soil, stone, and spirit at

Bollingen.[117] He chiseled, hammered, carved and cultivated the remnants and elements of the earth, and developed his spirit. By working in the soil, he worked within himself to discover the spirit within him. It is only in the earth from which we all herald that our spirit becomes the space between us.[118] The more we humbly cultivate our space the humbler we become. It is this humility in the presence of "grace"[119] that allows the emergence of unconditionality.[120] Until we can relinquish the glitter and glamor of conditionality for the *naked essentials of relation* we will never fully appreciate the emergence of spirit in relation.[121]

There is great solace in essentials. When we clutter our lives with all the inessentials of life we create the basis for conditionality. Everything that we do becomes a condition of something else. The *naked essentials of relation* are engendered by the simple act of being unconditionally present for the other[122] in silent regard. This opens the corridor of spirit and allows an uncontaminated symbiosis to emerge. We must remember that the unconditionality of being fully present for the other[123] is a closely knitted symbiotic relation. I think of Buber's "I-Thou"[124] relation almost as if it is encased in an amniotic relationship of one person to another. This unconditionality[125] creates freedom of thought and expression which often expresses itself manifesting as movement, gesturing and even playful activity. This is what I have termed "archetypal language."[126]

Archetypal language is the pre-verbal language that is expressed out of the deeper more archaic regions of our brain. It is the language that is most manifest when unconditionality[127] is present. When relation is steeped in unconditional presence[128] for another it generates a movement of deeper self-expression. In my original writings, I wrote about our "spatial field of optimal interaction"[129] and how I considered it a pivotal component of interpersonal dialogue. It is the space "in-between"[130] that we unconsciously cultivate for the free expression of our pre-verbal language, and that allows us greater access to our more archaic emotions. It is the space that reflects each person's psychic boundaries, and how these psychic boundaries are put in place when two or more persons come together for dialogue. I wrote this in relation to caretakers who needed to optimize their communications with ill, grieving, or emotionally troubled individuals. What I have since discovered is that this "spatial field of optimal interaction,"[131] and how one is given the freedom to navigate within this field, is the unconscious arena for deeper archaic expression. It is the arena where our interpersonal unconscious becomes a symbiotic participant in dialogue, and when that dialogue is grounded in unconditionality[132] it can evolve to the "I-Thou"[133] relationship. It is this deeper archaic self-expression that allows the more subterranean emotions and conflicts to emerge in selfless expression. When the *spatial field*[134] becomes the safe amniotic container for unconditional dialogue[135] it opens the door for deeper relation.[136] This is how we cultivate safe inner space.

Unconditional presence for the other[137] strips away the outer trappings of the world and creates a focused intention that only sees the other. Silence by the listener who attentively remains present for the other evolves into a poetic dance of eye movements and gesturing that begins to manifest the inner world of the person. This is *archetypal language*.[138] The inner person now emerges in the safe container[139] of the "psychic space."[140] This becomes the momentary holding environment[141] where unconditional presence[142] translates into unconditional acceptance of the other.[143] The other's inner space begins to emerge in the space "in-between"[144] as a safe holding environment[145] of transitional self-expression. In this sense "holding" becomes freedom. It is the freedom of inner knowing that can only be known when unconditional presence[146] is unequivocally conveyed. To strip oneself down to the essentials of relation is to be present.[147] We strip away all the pomp and glory and simply exist for the other in that moment. This is unconditional presence.[148] In that moment it is not psychology or philosophy, but simply "being present"[149] in the most complete way possible. It is the act of simply being there for the other person; being silent, listening, allowing the other to be. In Winnicott's concept of "holding" he noted the significance of knowing when to be silent.[150] Silence is a great therapeutic and personal tool that enables anyone to simply be present for the other.[151] We evolve from our silence to then reach out to the other and participate in the other's grief and suffering without losing ourselves and becoming a victim to the suffering.[152]

This is where "grace" in the "I-Thou" relationship[153] becomes the intangible factor that creates the aura of consoling depth that comes from somewhere outside us. It is that feeling or emotional depth that one knows has some basis outside of our sphere of function. This is the *spirit* "in-between"[154] It is the emergence of the intangible "grace" that Buber discusses in the process of relating.[155] It is the phenomenon of knowing when something is happening outside your sphere of personal experience, because it is an experience of spirit.[156] It is this experience of *spirit*[157] that I believe becomes the connecting link "in-between"[158] that makes unconditional presence[159] an *unconditional spirit* that is the "grace" that both transcends and connects us.[160] This is what makes each one of us capable of helping the other when the other's grief and suffering needs more than any one of us can give. We become unconditionally present,[161] and allow the spirit within us to become the spirit that binds us.[162]

We become a symbiotic expression of our unconditionality[163] for the other. Spirit emerges in the space that separates us, and then becomes the spirit in the space that connects us.[164] This is the spirit of embrace.

CHAPTER 1

THE SPIRIT OF EMBRACE

The first time I encountered the feeling that there was something special in the space between me and one of my patients, I was awestruck by the aura that seemingly enveloped us. My patient was a middle-aged woman who was deeply troubled, and somewhat overcome by a life that was filled with what she felt was personal failure and grief over the loss of her son to heroin. When I walked into the treatment room I saw her sitting in the corner of the room almost as if she was huddled in despair. The image I conjured was that of a skeleton sunken over in the chair with the weight of the world pressing on her shoulders. I gently greeted her as I knew this wasn't going to be an ordinary encounter, and I asked her if she was okay. Tears welled up in her eyes as her head dropped to her chest, and then she looked up at me. I slowly moved toward her and sat on the treatment table across from her chair, and just sat quietly. At that moment, there was a blanket of heaviness that engulfed our encounter, but suddenly this blanket began to lift.

She looked at me soulfully. Our eyes connected in a stream of quiet emotion almost as if there was a settling of the grief and despair she was feeling. This settling, however, took on a dimension of quiet solitude. It was a dimension that I could only think of as an intangible link that connected something between us and existed in the space that separated us. It was a vibrational link that somehow made ordinary space an extraordinary space.[165] I could sense that my body was feeling what her body was feeling in a way that went beyond what analysts would refer to as countertransference. It was *spirit*.[166] This is the only way that I could describe what was happening in the space that separated us.

At the time of our initial encounter, when I sat on the treatment table next to her, I had not yet uttered a word other than to greet her; however, in that moment of silence and sorrow there was the emergence of spirit.[167] This, I believe, is what Buber would term "grace."[168] It is knowing that something outside the reality of our ordinary space and time has emerged in the extraordinary space between us.[169] This spirit, however intangible it may be, creates a tangible vibrational link that unifies the soul of the unconditionally present person to the other.[170] In my experience this is not something that has to be sought in order to be found. It is the spirit that presides in each of us regardless of ethnicity, religion, race or creed.

In my writings I have used the term "archetypal dyad"[171] to depict the bond that occurs between two persons when they meet in unconditional relation.[172] It is a fusion of their unconscious psyches and it is their deeply focused intention that when *I encounter you I also encounter spirit*.[173] *Spirit* is the intangible "Thou" within us.[174] This is the way we discover the seed that connects us. When I interact with you, the ordinary space that separates us becomes the fertile soil that binds us, and for that moment in time we occupy extraordinary space. How would our world evolve if each of us took the responsibility to safeguard the space between us every time we meet? When I am unconditionally present for you[175] I allow extraordinary space to emerge in the space that separates us. I encounter you as you are at that moment, and in that moment, you become all the things you have always been.[176] You become present as a history of yourself,[177] and the space that separates us now embraces us. It is a *spirit of embrace* grounded in the fertile soil of unconditionality[178] that becomes the rooted vine connecting us. "I am the vine and you are the branches. . ."[179] is the soul of unconditionality. It is the spirit that embraces us every time I encounter you unconditionally. Spirit cannot exist without *us*.[180]

In the same way that we need *spirit* to bring the fruits of relation to life spirit needs us to be born and fulfilled in relation.[181] Without us the spirit in life dies.[182] This, perhaps, is God's greatest task for us. God comes to life in us and emerges in us as the vine that flows in the space between us. Without spirit, we are without unconditional relation because spirit is the essence of unconditionality.[183] Buber and Jung have elucidated these ideas from differing perspectives, but the theme is unchanged. We need God, but God also needs us to be realized in life.[184] I think it becomes equally important to extend this idea to include all living forms of life. Spirit is born in life, and it is not for anyone to judge how the value of life differs from one form to another. When I stand in relation to another it becomes my responsibility to be there unconditionally. If I value my life above any other life, at that moment I have made the other an "It" to paraphrase Buber.[185]

Ordinary space becomes extraordinary space in the spirit of embrace. It is not for me to decide when I am encountered if the life of a shivering dog is more important than mine or anyone else's. My only responsibility at that moment is to embrace the other unconditionally and enter the spirit of embrace. This is how we become the branches of the vine that bears the fruit of the spirit. When we begin to fully embrace the spirit between us we realize that all of life is precious, and that all life deserves unconditionality. When we unconditionally embrace each other we unconditionally embrace God.[186] This is how God comes to life in all those beings that possess life. Each time I fully encounter some other, and I become unconditionally present, I allow spirit to emerge.[187] My unconditionality becomes the foundation for the emergence of spirit through "grace."[188]

In "Psychology and Alchemy" Jung developed the theme of the creation of the new element. He discussed how the alchemists of old would mix two basic substances to produce the cherished third substance in the reaction.[189] This idea fits well in relation to the emergence of spirit when we unconditionally encounter each other in relation.[190] This is how ordinary space becomes transformed into extraordinary space and becomes the invisible branches of the vine. My soul enters relation with you, but only if my unconditional presence[191] opens that door.

Until I become present solely for you there is no "Thou" in the encounter.[192] We can only embrace spirit if spirit is rooted in our encounter. An example of this is best illustrated in one of my encounters with a patient just a few years after I entered private practice. I was just finishing my morning schedule one Saturday when I smelled the peculiar odor of kerosene. My receptionist hurriedly came into my office and told me I needed to come to the front desk immediately. Realizing something was wrong, I jumped up and made my way to the front desk. In one of our reception room chairs I noticed one of my patients soaked in kerosene and holding his cigarette lighter which was unlit. Calmly, I just said, "John, come into my office." He just looked at me, but after a few moments he got up and made his way to the corridor. As he approached, I simply put my arm around his shoulders and brought him into my office. We sat on our diagonally arranged conference chairs, and as we did he held up his lighter and said, "I'm going to set myself on fire; there's just no more reason for me to live."

At that moment, I knew he had every intention of carrying out his plan. He flicked the lighter which sparked, but didn't fully light, and as he did all I could think to do was to whisper his name. "John," I said, "Look at me." Slowly he lifted his eyes and looked at me, and something between us happened. As I looked into his eyes my body softened almost as if I was somehow cushioning the intense pain he was feeling. Slowly, as his eyes swelled with tears, I felt as if we were both stripped of all but our basic functions. It was just him and me sitting with an empty space between us. But there was more. Suddenly, he whispered an almost unintelligible word that I couldn't fully understand, so I leaned a little closer. "Thank you," he whispered, "Thank you for caring." With that John handed me the lighter which I carefully took from him and placed into my pocket. He slowly got up from his chair and walked over to me, and in his kerosene-soaked clothes he embraced me and let out the last of his sobs.

I couldn't help but wonder what transpired between us that ultimately led him to relinquish his thoughts about such a violent suicide. Certainly, I had not said anything beyond just a few words during our initial interaction that could have possibly led him to relinquish his thoughts of suicide. As I thought about it, however, it wasn't just what had transpired between us during that encounter, but it was all those past encounters we had that had led up to that point. That is what led John to my office in the first place. John was a young man who was always deeply troubled about his life, sexuality, and family. He often lived his life in ways that were less than admirable, but on the other hand, John had many redeemable qualities. He had a kind soul that always seemed to shine through some of his bleakest and more troubled moments. Whenever I met with John, I always tried to focus by totally engaging his every word and listening intensely to his message. Often, I would just remain silent as he pantomimed and engaged the space between us. But there was always something much deeper that I knew was going on in the background of our conversations.

Jung developed the idea that each of us has a "soul guide" within the deeper layers of our unconscious that helps us connect our ego functions to our often hidden and greater innate potential.[193] Each time I met with

John, we were able to forge an alliance between what was unconscious in him and what was unconscious in me. It was within the unconditional presence of our relation[194] that allowed the spirit in me to meet with the spirit in John. The "unconditional relation"[195] became the rooted vine from which the invisible branches of spirit crossed the bridge and connected us. When any person meets another in a time of utter human need, and the other becomes present unconditionally,[196] the vine of spirit becomes rooted. When we strip away all the trappings of egotism and become unconditionally humbled like the wounded soul before us, the divine branches of the rooted vine connect us.

This is how we encounter the *spirit of embrace*. It is the spirit in each of us that cannot be fully realized until it meets and joins with our inner soul-guide and some other's inner soul-guide.[197] Buber's unconditional presence is the soil upon which the *spirit of embrace* is born between us.[198] The soul in each of us becomes connected in the *spirit of embrace* when we become humbled by the suffering of another. If we are unwilling to become "meek and humble"[199] in the presence of another's suffering, and strip ourselves of our regalia and preoccupations, we will never open the doors that lessen the suffering of others. The *spirit of embrace*, we must remember, is first an embrace of our inner soul to the spirit within us, but also an embrace of our inner soul to the soul and spirit of the other who allows us to be unconditionally present[200] with them.

It is impossible to fully appreciate the immensity of life in the spirit of embrace. When I encounter someone in "unconditional relation"[201] I encounter the spirit in him in all its totality. This totality includes the world of the person in the same way that it includes the totality of my world. Buber discusses how this totality in the spirit, or in God, cannot be experienced outside of the world, or in the world for that matter. It must be experienced by apprehending the world in the person.[202] When I encounter all of you I encounter you in the spirit of embrace, and the spirit between us is what Buber would say is "... between I and You."[203] When I think about John and how he came to me that day, I recall vivid images of a man who had lost his way and couldn't find the spirit that animated his soul. His eyes were sunken and vacant, and the only thing that seemed to matter to him was the lighter that held the flame. It was the symbol of his self-destruction and typified the evil forces that had consumed the spirit that animated his soul. Buber tells us that the soul of the person never gets sick alone without there being a "between-ness" with some other.[204] I think this is a pivotal concept in understanding why the relationships we develop with others is so important. The soul of the person maintains life by the love that fuels it in its existing relationships with others. Buber eloquently examines this idea in "The Redemption of Evil,"[205] and shows us how it is our abiding love for individuals, not in the conceptual sense of loving humanity, but our 'concrete' love of people in our daily everyday dealings that is the true love of man.[206]

When John sat before me, I couldn't help but wonder about all those human relationships in his life that somehow extinguished the flame of *spirit* within him and allowed the flame of evil to emerge in his soul. It reminded me of Buber's discourse in "The Nature of Evil"[207] where he views good and evil as "existent states of human reality," and not as distinct polar opposites as they are most often considered.[208] In other words, it is our composite nature as human beings to exist in this dual state where we have the potential to perform acts of either reality. However, and I paraphrase Buber, when we turn our entire being toward God in what the Jews or Hassid call "Teshuvah" we reach out to God in His capacity and resolve for our "redemption."[209] What is most important in my view of this statement is that it is only through relation that we can ultimately encounter God's redeeming power.[210] We need to encounter God in some other that allows us to find God within ourselves.

In the act of relation, we enter the "archetypal dyad"[211] of my soul and your soul and enliven our spirit to sprout the branches of the vine that connect us; this is where we find the *Healing Spirit*. "Whenever any two or more gather in my name there I am among them."[212] The *healing spirit*, in my opinion, is the spirit in God that is the spirit in us. It is the divine sparks that the Zohar depicts as the mythical shower of God in all His living creatures.[213] It is not until the act of relation, however, that we find the *Healing Spirit* emerging in the space between us[214] to heal the soul within us. My concept of the "archetypal dyad"[215] attempts to depict our deeper unconscious connection that allows this spirit within us to become the spirit "in-between."[216] I introduced this term in my first book, *Language of the Archetype*,[217] and further developed it for practitioners of the healing arts who were interested in deepening their relationship with their patients. The "archetypal dyad" is the unconscious union of our deeper psyches that can only occur when unconditionality[218] is present. It is within this context that Jung's idea of the mixing of the *alchemical elements*[219] has relevance.

When I am fully invested in understanding you, I must, strip myself of all preconceived notions. I enter relation with you, and when I deepen our relation,[220] we cross the chasm that separates us. This can only happen when we metaphorically mix the alchemical elements of our souls. In alchemy, the alchemists mixed basic elements to produce the cherished gold of the reaction.[221] This becomes the rooted vine that slowly grows and unfolds the branches that connect us and eliminates the space that separates us. The "soul-guide" in me reaches out to the "soul-guide"[222] in you and allows spirit to emerge within the branches of the rooted vine. I think we underestimate the value of deepening our discourse with each other when we are in general conversation, and this is understandable. However, we need of necessity to sensitize ourselves to the subtle nuances and cues of each other that telegraph a need for deeper discussion. Our present environment, typified by our advances in telecommunications, has diluted our capacity to simply listen attentively to the other. This obfuscates our capacity and inclination to read what I have previously described as "archetypal language" which are all those non-verbal nuances of body movement and facial expression that become an active and ongoing catalogue of inner thought.

When I open myself to the other I become their symbiotic partner. I allow myself to simply listen, and through this simple act of compassion the other hears their own inner voice. They feel their emotion pass through their body, and unconsciously express thoughts that can't be spoken. They grimace, groan, frown, and posture what cannot be stated; but, in doing so, they start the process of unfolding their deeper conflicts and ambiguities. Within each of us there presides a "wise old man" and a "wise old woman"[223] silently waiting for our quiet appeal for guidance on our tumultuous path in life. These historical archetypes as they are called in Jungian psychology often come to us in dreams and reveries,[224] but are all too often dismissed as simple figments of our imagination. When we engage each other in compassionate interest we become the voice that summons these archetypes and draws them out of the unconscious domain.

Perhaps these archetypes are the lesser spirits of the kingdom that help guide us on our path to the "eternal Thou."[225] Are these the messengers of old? Are these the angels in our corner of the kingdom? Jung described archetypes in a similar vein to the angels depicted in the Judeo-Christian tradition, but as representations of the unconscious, and stressed how they should not be confused with the actual spiritual archetypes themselves.[226] These representations may come to us in dreams or visions as persons, personalities, spirits, images or symbols[227] with each one coming to us as our need arises.

One such symbol is the mandala wherein a circle is enclosed in a square and comes from the Sanskrit word meaning "magical circle."[228] It represents a quaternity where the number four is associated with wholeness and is often experienced in dreams as a symbol of integration and wholeness when our lives may be fragmented or chaotic.[229]

For instance, the "wise old man" or "wise old woman" are two such archetypal representations of our "personal unconscious."[230] The actual life force of these archetypes are unfathomable energies associated with the greater "collective unconscious" which lies outside our sphere of recognition.[231] One can't help but see the many parallels within the Judeo-Christian tradition of the prophets, saints, spirits, angels, and messengers that appeared to the prophets of old as depicted in both the Hebrew Bible and New Testaments. God needs us to be conscious of Him for Him to fulfill His mission for us, but we need God to fulfill our mission for being here. It is more realistic to see our spiritual unfolding within us as part of the universal plan on our path toward God.[232]

This idea, however, brings to light the need for both a personal inner process, and a more collective outer process to realize the fulfillment of our journey toward God. If spirit is to emerge in the space "in-between"[233] one's self and another it can emerge only because spirit lives in the soul of man. The process of dialogue may very well be the impetus that draws the rooted vine into the space that connects us, but the introspective process is what brings recognition of the spirit in man to life. Although Buber states that the spirit is not in man, and to paraphrase, is between himself and what he is not,[234,235] we all recognize a mystical part of ourselves that lies outside the functions of psychology and emotion, and close to what we would refer to as God or *spirit*.

In the primary Jewish Kabbalah text the Zohar the primordial spirit of God is depicted as being showered and raining down upon all His creation.[236,237] This is the spirit of God in man, and is the *Shekinah* as it is known in Jewish and Hassidic circles representing *God's spirit everywhere*.[238] If spirit is not in mankind than spirit is nowhere to be found. We can embrace the *Healing Spirit* between us because the other's unconditional presence opens our hearts and allows *spirit* to emerge.[239] The space between us is the bridge that must be crossed for the emergence of spirit to be fully present and encountered. We need the other in the same way that

God needs us to be fulfilled in the relationship of being.[240] Introspection is not enough for the fulfillment of spirit within us. We need the other to complete the cycle of God's creation, and in so doing, spirit is both recognized in us and through us.[241]

All through the ages mankind has used symbols and symbolic representations to express inner experiences that transcended both the spoken and written word. This is one of the origins of the mandala.[242] Human beings have traditionally evolved their innermost creative energies in the direction of art and symbolism because life as it is lived and experienced in the spirit cannot otherwise be drawn out. Although the physical expression of the inner spirit in art, poetry, dance, and symbolism is an effective way to engage the spirit within us, it cannot be fully encountered or embraced without encountering it in reciprocal relation.[243] This is the fundamental essence of what it means to be created in God's image. The spirit in God is the spirit in each of us, and enkindling spirit necessitates looking into the eyes of the other so that the rooted vine of spirit emerges in the space "in-between"[244] and connects us.

It is simply not enough to seclude oneself in silent meditation without leaving the confinement of the cushion to enter relation.[245] I am a firm believer in the life of the soul, and the beauty and magnificence of the meditative experience. It is through the quiet contemplation on the cushion that we experience the inner connection to the life force, and all it brings to us in our creative energies. However, life on the cushion, if it is to enliven the spirit within, cannot be fully embraced until it becomes a reciprocal force exchanged in the space "in-between."[246] The space that separates us is ordinary space until it is transfigured to extraordinary space by the unconditional presence of the other, and the emergence of the *Healing* Spirit between them.[247]

I often find that meaningful dialogue often leads to meaningful inner reflection. It is less important whether one first engages dialogue and then proceeds to meditation or the other way around. What I do find important is that the contemplative experience of inner reflection becomes joined with the reciprocal exchange with some other. Meditation can bring spirit to awareness, but we cannot embrace spirit until it is born in the other as we occupy ordinary space together. This, in my opinion, is the essence of Buber's reciprocity.[248]

CHAPTER 2

THE HEALING SPIRIT

One of my earliest experiences that helped me to understand the significance of a healing spirit was when I was in session with a woman who had recently lost her infant son to cancer. She was obviously in the deepest throes of emotional pain that I had ever encountered, and it humbled me to see her hurt so deeply. I couldn't help but feel the pangs of horror that rippled through her chest as she would describe the littlest of mannerisms that little Danny would enact. A simple smile or twitch of his lip became a cauldron of heart wrenching memories that she couldn't bear.

She would often hold her arms across her chest as she talked about him just as if she was holding him in her arms. During the time I was with her I was only in practice less than a year, and this experience became a pivotal event in my understanding of the depth of human suffering. It became the vehicle that activated an involuntary involution or turning within myself to try to find the hidden spirit that I knew had to be there; the spirit that might somehow lessen the suffering. Each time we talked I realized there was a little unfolding of some inner part of her that was trying to escape the confines of her pain. It was like an energy trying to burst forth from the confines of her inner cell.

Slowly over time I came to recognize that this unfolding was more than just the physical mannerisms of pain. There was a subtle movement developing between us that was becoming a hidden dialogue that I would come to describe as a "background pantomime."[249] Each of us began to unconsciously fill the space between us[250] as if we were metaphorically re-enacting our painful emotions. This language presented itself as an implicit dialogue that pantomimed our spoken word outside of our conscious recognition. Ultimately, I would come to realize that we were equally engaged in an unconscious dialogue where our inner selves were communicating with each other in a way that would cushion our more painful and hidden emotions. It seemed that the more we spoke and the more deeply we interacted the more focused and implicit the language became.

It is this *implicit*[251] evolution of unconscious language that I realized emanated from the deeper and more archaic regions of our brain. This was not "body language" as we commonly know it. Body language is an *explicit* series of mannerisms to which we have ascribed a pre-determined meaning, and which are generally under some conscious recognition. What I was experiencing with my patient was something outside the sphere of ordinary awareness. It manifested in an unconscious orchestration of movements that was often imperceptible to the naked eye. It wasn't until I so fully invested myself in trying to comprehend her pain that this reality came into focus. As time progressed I was able to see how both time and compassion were able to help her through the horrors of her loss. Much later however, I realized that there was so much more happening between us than just our spoken words. We had begun to share an "implicit" language that I much later termed *archetypal language*[252] when I was finally able to document the regions of the brain where I thought this hidden language was emanating.

This archetypal language is a manifest part of every one of us. It is that deeper more archaic language of self-expression that develops in our earliest stages of fetal development.[253] Unlike common body language that is often catalogued and ascribed a pre-determined meaning, this cannot be done to archetypal language which is stifled and inhibited when such practices are enacted. It is this indeterminate aspect of archetypal language that I believe is the unconscious movement of the spirit emerging in physical space as the *healing spirit*.

The more deeply we engage each other in dialogue the more we allow the deeper layers of our psyche and soul to unfold to each other. This unfolding is not something that can be learned. It is a process that can only be experienced in the practice of doing. There are no postures or body movements to learn or to catalogue, or any pre-determined movements to master. We simply meet the other person in dialogue with an unconditional presence[254] that allows the barriers that cover our soul to fade away. We become a focused participant stripping away our fleeting concerns to only be present[255] for the other.

Buber discussed spirit as being *between* the two persons in dialogue, and not being in the "I."[256] Spirit, in my opinion, emanates from the soul of mankind, and it becomes the essence of healing between and within us when it is freely expressed across the chasm that separates us. When I meet you in dialogue, and I can sufficiently strip myself of all those follies that commonly consume us, I enact an *implicit*[257] process that fills the space[258] that separates us. This *implicit* process[259] is part of an *archetypal language*[260] that I believe enacts a deeper meaning to the spoken word. David Bohm, the great theoretical physicist, developed the concept of the "implicate order" in which he described an underlying reality that was the emanating basis of all our outward experiences.[261] This is in large part how I believe the inner psyche unfolds in the chasm that separates us when we are deeply engaged. We strip away the outward reality and allow "spirit" to emerge from within. It is the spirit within us that finds its outward expression only when we are sufficiently engaged in an unconditional presence[262] with the other. It is this unconditional presence[263] that I believe unmasks the barriers that separate us and enacts the *implicit process*[264] that develops as *archetypal language*. It is this unmanifest order of David Bohm[265] hovering in the terrestrial landscape of our deeper psyche awaiting its moment of expression. It dances in the background of our every movement and occupies our every moment, but it is incapable of expression and recognition until we are unconditionally present for the other.[266]

When I encountered my patient's grief and suffering I was humbled by the depth of her loss. Her grief and suffering stripped away all the barriers that shielded my soul and cluttered the space that separated us. This *implicit transition* from *explicit dialogue* to *implicit dialogue* created closure of the psychological chasm between us. It symbiotically freed our self-expression and began to free our body's repressed pain and sorrow.[267] I often think back to the many conversations I have had when the person I was speaking with was suffering. I can immediately recall when our *explicit dialogue* began to transition to *implicit dialogue*. The person would enact unconsciously generated movements that would become their personal signature of how they suffered. We open the door to the *implicit process*[268] by opening ourselves to the suffering of the other. When we open ourselves sufficiently we allow the "grace" that Buber discussed to bring forth the spirit that fills the space between us.[269]

When I encounter the other in this depth of implicitness I begin to transition our dialogue to a deeper order. It is here, within us and in the space between us,[270] where the spirit[271] of an *implicate order*[272] presides. David Bohm introduced the idea of an "implicate order"[273] in his discussion of quantum physics. It is the underlying field from which we grasp little particulate experiences that we commonly associate with our everyday lives. When I so deeply engage you in dialogue that we transcend our explicit reality, we enter the stream of the "implicit process." It is here, in the implicate matrix between and within us, that the healing spirit presides.

It is always amazing to me when I think about some of the encounters I have experienced with my patients, and how our dialogue evolved when our encounters deepened. Previously, I have written about one of my patients who suffered untold childhood traumatisms. As a young child, she was victimized by her older siblings who at one point threw her down a flight of stairs damaging her spine. In one of our encounters when she was describing the pain that she suffered from this event I found myself holding my hands together in front of my chest as if I was holding a sphere within my hands. This posture softened her. She unknowingly gazed at my hands and said, "You're holding the egg." I realized that it looked like I was holding an egg, but at that moment the egg implicitly became a therapeutic container that centered her in ways that were not explicitly knowable.

This is the *implicit process*.[274] Spirit emerged between us[275] because it came to life within us. There is something about our suffering that somehow serves as a prerequisite to our redemption and reconciliation within the spirit. Until we are willing to fully encounter the other in all their suffering and humanness we deny ourselves the opportunity to bring them to the *healing spirit* within and between us. Buber makes the point that we cannot enact the process of unconditional relation if we are unwilling to encounter the other as the other is.[276] I must be fully present and encounter the other in their totality and all their human imperfections.[277] This engages the human spirit.

We live in an age that has become a confused mixture of gadgets, and although there is much benefit to the "cloud" of technology that we now enjoy, there is much risk of losing something much greater. Human beings need each other on a deeply human level to live and survive as people. When I embrace you, I do so as one person to another, and in that moment of embrace there is spirit and grace.[278] When we talk, and I engage you, I close the chasm between us, and I encounter all those things about you in the reality of that moment.[279] Unfortunately, our new "cloud" of technology all too often removes the reality of our encounter in the buzz and glitter of the gadgets that consume our world. This, I believe, is the great risk of the present day. It is not a question of whether we need to advance our technology, but how we can advance it without losing our souls in the process.

The healing spirit can only heal in the spirit of healing. Human beings need each other on a deeply human level to engage those inner energies that become our stream of connectedness. It is this stream of connectedness that joins us when either one of us deeply cares for the other. This is what opens the door to the healing spirit and closes the chasm between us. I cannot open that door if we are not fully present[280] to each other and this is the risk of the present day. If you are not "here" when I am here for you, we regress to an anonymous relationship. Connectedness requires duality before it can progress to unity. At a minimum, one of us must at least be present for us to fully and unconditionally encounter the other.[281]

Once again, there is great solace in naked essentials. I often think of relation as a process of stripping away the outer trappings to reach the inner soul of connectedness. This is the stream of connectedness that becomes the branches on the vine[282] that brings duality to unity. We begin as two and then evolve to the unity that can only occur when I become humbled by our encounter. It is this idea that I believe actualizes the spirit within to become the spirit in-between.[283] This is also why I feel that Jung contributed a pivotal part of this process by introducing the transcendent function.[284] When we evolve ourselves to our higher function we can evolve beyond the preoccupations of the ego and engage spirit.

Spirit, however, can only emerge between us when it is a manifestation of spirit within us. The healing spirit is the very ground substance of what all the mystics have tried to identify within them. It is their Kundalini, the coiled female energy within them, that intertwines the depth of their being. To the Christian it is the comforter of Christ's Holy Spirit within them, and the life force that drives their lives. This is the divine interplay of inner and outer energies that find expression when we subjugate our ego driven forces to the reorganizing drive of spirit. I think this idea can be brought into focus by looking at the dynamics of Christ and His apostles at the Last Supper.

Christ sat among his apostles. Each of them was separate and distinct from the other and preoccupied with the suffering and death that was upon them. The talk centered on the immanent. Christ was going to be tortured, crucified and buried, and the apostles would be left to carry on the work before them. Ultimately, they would suffer a great deal on His behalf even to the point of death and crucifixion. Among the apostles there would also be the one who would betray their Lord and send him to His crucifixion and death. But then there was the *bread and wine*. The bread and wine became the body of interconnectedness that entwined the separate and disparate energies of the scared and frightened apostles to the unity that made them one with their Lord. The *bread and wine* evoked the spirit within each of them that ultimately would emerge as the divine spirit in the space that separated them. The bread and wine of Christ became the body and soul of relation.[285] This was the symbolic act of interconnectedness that would become the actual life of divinity within them. We also find the presence of the inner spirit depicted in the ancient medieval text of Jewish mysticism known as the Zohar. This spirit was depicted in the Zohar[286] as the raining down of the divine spirit upon and within the exiled people of Israel to become the Shekinah of Judaism.[287]

The Shekinah is the term that was used by the ancient Jewish rabbis to depict the ever-indwelling presence of God.[288] Shekinah is the *ever-present* divine spirit both within and amid the people. As the female counterpart to God she is within them to both protect and to participate in their suffering.[289] Shekinah is the spirit within the human soul.[290] It is the foundation of the healing spirit within us that can reach out like the branches of the vine to become the stream of connectedness that closes the chasm between us. This divine spirit is the naked essential of the soul. It is the divine energy that we have buried beneath the layers of chaos and confusion that separates us. This chasm can only be closed when spirit emerges in the "in-between"[291] from within each of our souls. I think the greatest gift we have as human beings is the gift of choice. We can ultimately choose to participate in the divine reality that is a part of each of us. When I meet another, I choose. I make a choice to either encounter you or to stand behind the veil of conditionality. When I encounter you, I participate in *the bread and wine of relation* which means that I am willing to suffer with you. It is this aspect of one's dialogue with another that I believe is the fundamental basis of dialogue. All dialogue is risk. Each time we meet we engage each other in a process of choice. In the most fundamental sense we choose to either allow the opportunity for meaningful exchange to occur, or we choose to rest our words in the realm of superficiality.

Superficiality has its place in the world. This is Buber's world of the "I-It" relation[292] and we need to recognize that this is a reality that allows us to effectively navigate in the world. Obviously, we need to have conditions within the objective world to live. We need to plan our day, eat our breakfast, drive our cars, and generally safeguard ourselves from the dangers of the world. However, there is a choice to be made. Each moment that I navigate in the world there is choice. I must choose to be fully present[293] whenever I encounter another, or I preclude the spirit of relation. Meaningful dialogue requires awareness of when I have become inattentive to you.

The world order is the world of "I-It."[294] Jesus, in the Christian tradition, was from a Kingdom not of this world. The kingdom of this world as we know it today is too often the world of the moneychangers and charlatans. Our world has exploded into an arena where meaningful dialogue is obscured by the ever-present bombardment of electronic media and gadgetry. Meaningful dialogue is contingent, first and foremost, on a willful desire for meaningful exchange. The greatest threat to suffocating the healing spirit within and between us is to forget that it is there. Perhaps it is time to relinquish our grip on all the gadgets that have so overly constellated our attention, and once again choose to be present.

CHAPTER 3

THE BREAD AND WINE OF RELATION

I remember as a young boy how important it was for us to always have dinner as a family. We were a Catholic Italian family living in a predominantly Italian Catholic neighborhood of aunts, uncles, cousins and friends who lived there most of their lives. Each night at about six o'clock, my two sisters and I would sit patiently at the table as my mother prepared the final trappings, and my father prepared to sit at the table. As we gathered around the table amidst the clanking of our forks and spoons, my mother would fill our plates and bowls with the pasta that was the staple of so many of our traditional dishes.

As the food was passed and served from one of us to another, we each would jump in and out of endless conversations. Often, the cacophony of our voices and the clanging of our plates and bowls was deafening, but amidst all this activity I would often gaze upon our table. Just off from the center of the table, and near my father's place, was the bottle of red wine and the loaf of crispy Italian bread that decorated each evening's meal. From time to time each of us was given a sip of the red wine as the bread was freely pulled from the loaf and passed around the table. Somehow, the bread and wine were there in a way I didn't fully understand, and it was present in a way that seemed to connect us as a family and as a culture. In many ways, the bread and wine were part of the soil under our feet. It was fruit from the vine that we made from the fresh purple grapes of the earthly vineyard. It was part of the earthly soil upon which we trod. I remember how my grandfather would always break a piece of the bread and tell me to dip it in the wine. "Sweet," he would say, "sweet." And it was sweet, but what was more important to me than the sweetness of the bread and wine, was the simple act of dipping the bread into the wine.

There was something about this simple act that seemed to transcend the act itself. It wasn't until much later that I came to realize how the bread and wine on the table between us was also the bread and wine of our relation. The bread and wine closed the space between us and became the vine that connected us. The bread and wine were our symbolic center of relation. I remember as a boy how the local priest would come to our house during the month of May to pray the rosary. It was a neighborhood tradition to honor the Blessed Mother, and all my aunts and uncles and cousins would gather after dinner for the prayer. My cousins and I usually sat on the floor while my aunts and uncles and my parents usually sat on chairs or knelt in front of the statute of Mary. When we finished praying the rosary, my father would take the bottle of wine and whatever kitchen glasses we had and put them in the center of the table. It wasn't long before Father Lidossi or Father Prastora and my father and uncles were sitting at the table, and my mother and aunts were getting the Italian bread and cold cuts for a little after dinner gathering. The bread would be broken, the wine poured, and the glasses raised, and the simple act of sharing had begun.

These were the *naked essentials of relation*. There was something very deep and personal about this simple act of breaking the bread and pouring the wine. The wine was the fruit of the vine that we made from the fresh purple grapes we squeezed every spring. It was part of our soil. It was the life blood of our extended family, and the soil upon which our ancestors trod before us. With the sharing of the bread and wine there was community, and although our family was not spared the trials and tribulations of daily life, that sense of community was always there. As I grew older, I would come to understand that the naked essentials that embodied this simple act of sharing also embodied the process of relation on a much deeper level. The bread and wine of relation was a fundamental state of our reality. In its most symbolic form it was the bread and wine of Christ. This reality coursed through our veins and became the branches of the vine that connected us. It is unfortunate how we have lost so many of our family traditions in our present world. The simple act of sitting at the family dinner table and engaging in relation is all but lost in the chaotic arena of daily life.

There is something very special about a mother feeding her children and a father taking his seat at the dinner table. This simple act of preparing and serving the night time meal, and then partaking in all its pleasures is a foundation of relation. The simple act of breaking the bread becomes an act of relation when I break it for you. This is the continuity between you and I that is carried forth into the greater world. We learn to make even the most mundane acts of daily life a hallowing[295] experience by sharing in the fundamental goodness of relation.

There was a time in our society when what we did in the family and at the dinner table served as the basis for what we did in the greater world. Today, it is the greater world that determines what we do in the family and at the dinner table. The simple act of relation is now all but lost to the preoccupation with cell phones blaring in between bites and texting the next important message. It is no wonder that our children are lost. At some point, we stopped appreciating the naked essentials of simply being present[296] for each other and substituted the pomp and folly of neurotic consumerism in its place. Family tradition and the simple act of breaking the bread and sipping the wine needs to be reexamined.

Buber elaborated on the unifying nature of the soil, and how it was lost when the Jews were exiled.[297] It is the common soil upon which we trod that unifies our soul[298] and allows us to maintain our continuity with each other in the world. This is the basis of our life in the world. We create a self-imposed exile by fleeing from the soil[299] of our way of life. It is important for us to recognize that the soil upon which we stand cannot be separated from our soul and spirit.[300] This is the fertile soil within which we become fully actualized as human beings and can produce good fruit. At some point we must consider how much we have lost by accelerating headlong into the technological arena. We have become enamored by the glitter of the gold, and the desire for instantaneous gratification of our needs. In the process, however, we have lost much.

The bread and wine of relation is a unifying act of solidarity. When I pull a piece of the bread from the loaf and hand it to you, I participate in nourishing body and soul. This symbiotic act becomes the instrument of relation. I am not advocating a return to the past, nor am I advocating that we eliminate our technological accomplishments. What is necessary, however, if we are to engender a healing spirit, is that we return to the fertile soil of communal and interpersonal relation.[301] Each time I trod upon the common soil with you, and accept you in relation, we partake in the bread and wine. We reduce the outer trappings, strip away the folly, and partake in the spirit of relation.[302]

I once had occasion to talk to a middle-aged woman, Mary, who had recently suffered the loss of her mother. I was told that she was quite depressed and had become somewhat reclusive a couple of months after her mother passed. One day about two or three months after Mary's loss, I was walking into our local café to buy a cup of coffee when I ran into her. I could see she was distraught as she had this constrained look on her face like her body was riddled with anxiety. When I looked at Mary I could see her eyes swell with tears. After offering my condolences, I asked her if I could buy her a cup of coffee and she agreed. We found a quiet corner of the café and quietly sat for a moment before she looked up at me from her cup.

As I looked into her eyes I could feel the depth of emptiness in her soul. Almost at that very moment she moved her hand from her cup and touched her heart. "I feel like I've lost so much," she cried. "First the breast cancer, now my mother." It was just three years before that Mary was diagnosed with breast cancer and had to undergo a radical mastectomy. Following her surgery, she then went for breast reconstruction which took quite a toll on both her mental and physical reserves. I sat silently. Mary quietly clutched her cup as she spoke about the pain in her heart and the emptiness that she felt. I clutched my cup and noticed that we both held our cups encircled in our hands in the space between us. In my mind, I imagined it was like a picture on a wall of two people in quiet conversation. The two cups that we held between us reminded me of "the imaginary egg" that I carefully cradled in my hands as I consoled my abused patent sometime before. It was the container that held the fragile spirit.

As Mary spoke we both slowly began to sip our coffee, and somehow the space between us seemed to lighten. "I've lost my mother," she cried, "and I need to know if we'll ever be together again." I knew Mary was a devout Christian, but at this moment of grief all she felt was the emptiness of loss. "Mary," I said, "we never really die;[303] we only suffer the pain of separation. I know that one day we'll all be together, and we'll all understand." Mary paused momentarily and slowly closed her hands around her cup. "I don't know," she whispered, "I hope so, but I don't know." As we sipped our coffee I noticed that Mary seemed a little better. Her body seemed to relax, and our conversation took on a more relaxed tone. Once again,

I imagined that picture in my mind of the two people in quiet conversation in the café. The picture changed. I imagined it in brighter colors and in a more jovial and friendly space. I wondered to myself how much of our unconscious dialogue had created this change in her. Unconsciously, we cradled our cups, sipped our coffee, held each other's gaze, and shared our common space in ways that seemed more meaningful than our words. I wondered if this was the case.

I once again thought about the bread and wine of relation. This archetypal language that symbolically expresses what our conscious minds cannot comprehend or fathom at the time. I thought about all those circuits in our brain that generate all that activity, but I still couldn't answer that one fundamental question. It seemed to me, however, that Mary needed to embrace her healing spirit. She needed to unlock the door that would allow the spirit within her to emerge in the space between us[304] like the branches on the vine. This is the *bread and wine of relation*. At the table this symbolic act of relation engendered the spirit of healing. Mary was able to take in the cradled cups between us and the subtle gazes of our eyes and allow our spirits to connect in space. I couldn't help but think about the words of Jesus when he said, "for where there are two or three gathered in my name there am I in the midst of them."[305] Each act of kindness becomes a symbolic act of relation when we maintain our awareness on the other. The cups that occupy the space between us, the bread that we share, and the wine that we sip are more than transitional objects[306] once we devote ourselves to the other person. Each object becomes the body and soul of relation.[307]

There is great significance in what is between us. When I devote myself to you in dialogue I create a vibrational link between us that opens a space within me. This inner psychic space is the healing space within me that opens the door between us and transforms ordinary space into extraordinary space. Whatever chasm lies between us will slowly begin to close as the bread and wine of relation enacts a reciprocity[308] that connects us. This "give and take" of relation loosens the binds of relation and begins to open the psychic space of the other person. This opening of the psychic space or loosening of the layers of our hidden defenses becomes the vibrational bridge that connects us. It is the symbolic bread and wine of relation that becomes the tangible spirit[309] between us. The spirit of relation[310] that Buber described is the spirit within each of us whose body and soul emerges and becomes our vibrational link. This is what requires "grace."[311]

Every time we open ourselves to each other in serious dialogue we create an unconscious invitation to engage the healing spirit between us. This healing spirit, however, can only emerge from the spirit that presides within each of our hearts and souls.

Life in the spirit is the life that acknowledges the spirit within each of us. When we open ourselves to each other in caring and devoted dialogue we engage each other beyond our tangible reality. We give ourselves the opportunity to actualize what may lie hidden beyond our scope of understanding. There is no greater way to experience God than to experience that ineffable source in another person. When the body lightens, the face enlivens, and the grimace becomes a smile in the space between you and the other person; you touch the bread and wine of relation. You know that you and the other person are more than the space you occupy.

There is something very special in the devotional quality of dialogue when it strips away the pomp of superficiality. It sets the stage for the emergence of spirit from deep within our souls. This is what I believe the great yogis discussed in relation to Kundalini and the chakras. The Kundalini in yogic tradition is the female goddess that lies within our inner germinal centers as the coiled serpent.[312] This is once again another depiction of the spirit within each of us. In Kundalini, the coiled goddess is the spirit or primordial energy that ascends within us from the depths of our inner pelvis to the height of the crown where our spiritual awakening presides.

It is spirit within the subtle manifestations of our body that is the integrating force that connects us. I have often found that when I am deeply invested in listening to another person, and I begin to unequivocally recognize that we have invisibly connected, there is a presence of spirit. Our space becomes vibrational in a way that moves the heart. In Kundalini, this is the essence of the heart chakra where spirit is symbolized as "air"[313] and becomes the higher expression of the energy within us. When I encounter this experience, I am always humbled by the great power of spirit. It is the spirit that presides in every cell of our body and enlivens the space within us. It is our "psychic space" and is the home of the *healing space* within and between us. It is the bread and wine of relation.

Each time we devote ourselves to listening to another we take the first step in enlivening the healing spirit within us. We take the risk of opening space and transforming ordinary space into extraordinary space for the benefit of the other person. There is no greater way to offer oneself in dialogue than to open our space to them. We become present by becoming humbled in the spirit. We must strip ourselves to the naked essentials of being and release the pomp and circumstance that consumes our daily lives.

The most important aspect of dialogue when we engage another person in the healing space is silence. Silence allows the other person to unfold the psychic space within them and begin the process of navigating the uncharted territory of extraordinary space. When we focus on the other person within the space between us we allow the vibrational link of spirit to emerge. This is the healing spirit. It is the yogis' Kundalini, and what all the great prophets and mystics have tried to define since the beginning of humankind. For me personally it is the Holy Spirit within each of us. It is the heart and soul of relation and becomes the spirit between us like the branches of the vine.

This is the bread and wine of relation. When you sit in relation, it doesn't matter if the cups between you and the other, the glasses on your table, or the plates that hold your food are anything more than the ordinary objects of the everyday. They become part of the vibrational link that allows the intangible to be grasped and molded in the space between you. This is "archetypal language" engaging spirit. We need only be present[314] to allow our inner spirit the freedom to mold our thoughts and fears in space. This is how the ordinary space that separates us becomes the extraordinary space that helps us to heal.

CHAPTER 4

THE MONASTIC SPIRIT

In all human dialogue, there is always a self-serving function that protects our persona and insures that our words and demeanor represent how we wish to be perceived. As I am now in the latter part of my career which has spanned some thirty-eight years of service in chiropractic, psychotherapy, and life coaching I have witnessed an evolution in interpersonal dialogue. I think the biggest change I have witnessed in my work with patients during this time is what I refer to as the monastic spirit of relation. I have always been intrigued by the great monastics of religious life. The Catholic monks and priests, Buddhist priests, and although not monks per se, the great Judaic thinkers like Maimonides, Buber, and Heschel. They always seemed to bring to *relation* a monastic toughness that centered them in their dialogue with others. Having been raised a Catholic, and having attended Catholic schools through High School, I often had occasion to dialogue with priests and nuns alike.

During one of my high school years when I was going through a typical adolescent crisis, I experienced this kind of monastic toughness that simply cut through the thicket of emotion and centered me. I was sitting in Father Salerno's office across a desk that he sat behind. He sat quietly with one leg crossed over the other and his hands folded in his lap. "So, you finally came in to talk to me," he said. I think those were the last words he said for about fifteen minutes. He was tough by reputation, and simply sat quietly as I absorbed his presence in our encounter. His eyes never left mine, and this seemed to center me more than I could accomplish at that time.

He was silent, but his silence was animated by his emotion and compassion, and this somehow seemed to fill the space between us.

As I look back, I think this very well may have been the beginning of my understanding of what I would later call *archetypal language*. Father Salerno's presence, and his demeanor, talked to me in ways that no amount of words could ever convey. There was an unconscious connection that bridged the chasm between us. It was the spirit in him connecting with the spirit in me. There were times during our conversations that I could almost see this bridge between us, and how it connected our souls in conversation. He was focused in ways that ordinary conversation wasn't focused. He was able to be there in body, mind, and spirit, and it was the totality of his presence that conjured and evoked body, mind, and spirit in me.

The evolution of spirit only occurs when it is joined in the spirit of some other. Father Salerno became the other that allowed my spirit to emerge, and during simple dialogue our spirits embraced. This is the *healing spirit*. It is impossible to understand the emotional equilibrium that occurs from silent exchange. When we engage in the silence of dialogue we encourage a monastic spirit that is centered in the soul of each of us. We become an open cell for the other to spill whatever needs to be poured from the deep recesses of their mind and soul. We accept them and their plight in the totality of who they are at that moment in time. Like Father Salerno we sit back and absorb the pain and suffering of the other without becoming a victim to the process.

Perhaps there is a certain mental toughness that is required in this process, and maybe that is why I use the word "monastic" in this regard. It is never easy to just "be" as opposed to "do." If there is one thing I have learned it is that *being* is often more important than *doing*. When we can become sufficiently focused to let the other become our only immediate interest then we have encountered the monastic spirit of relation. We strip away everything but the naked essentials of relation and "be." When I think back to my sessions with Father Salerno I most vividly recall his relaxed and focused interest in what I had to say. He never gave me the impression that anything I said was unimportant or of little interest to him. I feel fortunate to have had this experience because I learned firsthand the importance of focusing on the other person to the exclusion of all other preoccupations.

To be connected in the space that separates us means that we fully invest ourselves in the life of the other person, and it is this investiture that closes that chasm. The chasm closes, and we experience extraordinary space. We become linked participants in dialogue and experience the oneness of true relation. This is exactly what I experienced in those early encounters with Father Salerno. Each time I left our sessions I felt that I was understood, and that my concerns and feelings were validated. The most integral periods, however, were those times when I was simply received as opposed to questioned or interrogated. It was his presence in our encounter that was most important. Somehow, something filled the space between us and created a fundamental change in me.

All too often in the process of dialogue we feel prompted to animate and interject instead of listening. I often think about listening as an inward retreat that allows the other person to expand their inner self into outward space. This unfolds the process of deeper communication and allows deeper inner dialogue to occur. When we reach the point that we can inwardly control our tendency to violate our silence we open this door. It is this self-control in the process of dialogue that establishes the inner parameters that allows unfolding to occur. This is the archetypal dyad[315] that occurs when the inner unconscious or spirit of one person is linked to the inner unconscious or spirit of the other person.

The monastic spirit of relation filters out the noise between us by silencing the noise within us. We retreat into the inner cell of our being to free the other person from our preoccupations. One of my patients once commented to me about how her psychotherapist was constantly flitting about during their session. "It was like she was everywhere but here," she said. She told me how safe and confident she was in our sessions because, she said, "your eyes never leave mine; you're always right here."

This is what I mean by the monastic spirit. It is a self-controlled, disciplined communication that strips away all but the naked essentials of relation. You know that I am there with you because you are the only one that is there with me. This is the focused intention that centers the other person in a direct line of dialogue across the space between them. This ultimately closes the chasm and becomes the link that connects you and the other. This is how ordinary space becomes extraordinary space. It is an evolution of the spirit between and within each of those in dialogue when the dialogue is centered on the other.

I use the term *monastic spirit* in the true sense of the term. It reminds me of the spirit and devotion that is often required to penetrate through the pomp and preoccupations of our mind when we engage in serious dialogue. Perhaps this is why the monastics make a daily practice of prayer and meditation before engaging in their outer duties and responsibilities. The idea of *devotion in dialogue* might seem somewhat misplaced, but this term more accurately describes what is often necessary to penetrate the grief and despair of the suffering other. All too often our psychotherapies, counseling, coaching and interpersonal dialogues are cluttered in superficialities that fail to penetrate to the inner spirit of the person.

Grief and suffering require a devotion in dialogue that brings the listener to an inner appreciation of the other's suffering. It is this focused concern that constellates the unfolding of the spirit and allows the *implicit*[316] mind to emerge. This is when body language transitions to archetypal language, and all the subtle facial nuances, quiet unintelligible whispers, and clandestine expressions that date back countless generations emerge. One of my patients who was suffering the loss of her father was talking to me about how much she missed her father who had recently passed and left behind her cold detached mother. Each time she spoke with me I noticed that her lips always expressed this frown of consternation that sometimes seemed out of context to our discussion. This woman had a horrible relationship with her mother whom I had also known for a short time. The more I met with her, however, the more I realized that this was the same facial expression that her mother expressed every time she was upset with her daughter. At one point in our discussion I gently asked her about it. "I notice that you occasionally frown, Jane; what is that?" This question momentarily surprised her, but after a minute of introspection she began to nod her head like she had come to understand. She realized that there was more to her grief than her own sorrow because her sorrow also reflected the failed relationship between her father and mother. "My mother is never too far away from me," she said, "even when she isn't here."

This is archetypal language. It is a generational language that is as much a part of our genetic code as it is the learned behaviors of those whom we unconsciously introject into our psyche. This is why it is so important to engage the other person fully. It is only when the pomp and folly is peeled back that the *devotion in dialogue* can engage the inner core of the person generationally. This monastic spirit in dialogue penetrates through the layers of superficiality, and through the reciprocity of verbal speech and archetypal language the inner conflict is reconciled.

That one facial expression in my patient was literally worth a thousand words of dialogue. It painted a picture of a life torn between love and hate, joy and sorrow, and the unrealized dreams of a child who never knew the love of a caring mother. The idea of *devotion in dialogue* or the *monastic spirit* should not be misconstrued to think that interpersonal dialogue is somber or constrained. True interpersonal dialogue rests on a foundation of spontaneity. When we are engaged in the spirit we become animated in the spirit based on need and circumstance. Our laughter, cries, joys, and sorrows are reflected in our conversation and archetypal language.

When we devote ourselves to the other person in dialogue we respond to the person in the full context of being present.[317] This is what makes the dialogue real and spontaneous. I often think about dialogue like an exercise in the ancient forms of Tai Chi. We move in relation to each other like a dance across the vibrational string that connects us. We engage both the *explicit and implicit*[318] mind and allow freedom of expression across the space between us. Once the body moves, the face quietly animates or grimaces, and the chasm closes, we are then in unconditional relation.[319]

Our present-day culture has lost much of what I would term monastic. We fill the space between us with inessential barriers that take us away from each other in countless ways. We look at cell phones, computer screens and countless other media instead of looking at each other. It is a sad commentary to life being lived in the present. It is not my contention that these media should be discarded, but only that they find their proper place in our lives. One of my patients recently commented to me that his wife had to have her cell phone at the table each evening during dinner. She kept it next to her knife and fork in case her seventeen-year-old son who worked in a local supermarket might need her. Her husband became increasingly upset when he realized that she was more interested in sending texts to her co-workers than awaiting the never to be received call from her son.

I often wonder how many conversations we now miss because of our preoccupation with social media. We need to rethink our present path so that we can once again find each other in dialogue. I need to see you to receive you. I need to look into your eyes to feel what you feel. I cannot be there for you in your moment of grief and sorrow, in the full context of my being, if we do not share space together. This is the foundation of true dialogue. This does not preclude the use of electronic media when distance separates us, but this is a completely different circumstance. We need to separate ourselves from the neurotic preoccupation that presently consumes Western society and allow it to find its rightful place in our lives.

We need to once again look into the eyes of the other for the *devotion in dialogue* to become manifest, and this may require a little of the monastic spirit to be accomplished. I often speak of engaging dialogue in the "naked essentials" of our thoughts. Unless we are willing to strip away the frivolities of our ego to nakedly express our soul in dialogue we will miss the point entirely.

One of my colleagues who had read my previous book, *The Healing Space*,[320] asked me how many people I thought were capable of dialogue in the devotional sense that I was advocating. This question caught me by surprise. It made me realize how much we have lost in our capacity to simply be present for each other. I pondered this question for a moment, and then simply said what I felt was the truth. "We're all capable," I said. She looked at me with a distant soulful look in her eyes like I was taking too much for granted, and then turned away. My final thoughts as she turned away?

"We're all capable."

CHAPTER 5

JASON'S SORROW

One of the most sorrowful encounters I have had in clinical practice was a conversation I had with a veteran of the Vietnam War. When Jason was nineteen years old the Vietnam War was at its peak, and like others his own age, he was filled with a sense of pride at the thought of defending his country against what was touted as the fight against aggression and Communism. Jason's father and uncles all served in one capacity or another in the armed forces, and this served as a motivating drive to enlist himself in the army to defend his country.

Jason found himself amidst some of the most horrible encounters imaginable. He was engaged in numerous hand to hand combat situations, and often had to kill or be killed in numerous encounters with the enemy. Unfortunately, on one such occasion, Jason oversaw a squad that had to enter the thicket of the jungle to engage the enemy. Due to a miscalculation in the air support that his squad was supposed to have received, Jason and his squad were pummeled by the enemy. The way Jason explained it, there were bullets flying, bombs blasting, and soldiers falling everywhere. Flashes of light exploded and filled the thick air around them with smoke and fire in every direction. But then the worst happened.

Jason's best friend was struck by explosive fire. His abdomen was torn in half as his body shook on the blood-filled ground he lied upon. Almost as if by instinct, all Jason could think to do was to put the contents of his abdomen back into his stomach and call for a medic. But no medic came.

Jason picked up his friend and carried him in his arms as far as he could as bombs fell everywhere. As the bombs fell and the fire raged, Jason just kept running hoping that help would arrive to help him save his friend. But help never arrived.

Something inside Jason died that day, and the memory of his best friend lying in his arms dying was a memory that haunted him every day that he lived. As we sat and talked, the one thing that haunted Jason almost as much as his best friend dying, was the fact that he didn't die in the encounter with him. It wasn't that he just didn't die, but that he couldn't understand how he could have survived. As bombs fell and bullets whizzed by his head he was never once struck. On one occasion, he heard a bullet whiz by his ear. Jason wanted to die in exchange for his friend's life, and if he couldn't die in exchange for his friend's life then he wanted to die with his friend.

This was not meant to be. Jason would live the rest of his days in sorrow. He would live with the images of that day almost as if they were happening today, and there was no secret way to lessen the pain that he felt. It is during times such as these that we must become the vessel within which the person can openly express his implicit emotions. More importantly, perhaps, is that we also become the vessel upon which the person can subtly recreate or reenact his silent unconscious emotion in outward space. During our session, I watched as Jason unconsciously grasped his abdomen and clawed at his chest almost as if he was gasping for air like his buddy. My silent empathy, which was deeply heartfelt, opened the space between us and enabled him to pantomime what he felt but couldn't say. It was his implicit language. This was Jason's archetypal language emerging from the implicit regions of his soul to help him convey what was unimaginable.

What Jason couldn't say in verbal speech he expressed in the subtle nuances of his body that had nothing to do with what would commonly be called body language. His implicit mannerisms erupted from the deeper layers of his psyche as subtle nuances that might be easily overlooked in ordinary conversation. Most importantly is that the environment for this implicit dialogue be cultivated to open the space *in-between*[321] as opposed to interpreting the implicit mannerisms. It is the other who needs to create, mold, pantomime and grimace what is meaningful to them but can't be stated.

Once the other begins to evolve his grief into outward space the implicit or archetypal language will generally begin to manifest. The tugging of a button, the unconscious gripping of the arm of the chair, the silent quivering of the lip, all become the other person's implicit language. We are the vessel in outward space. In the same way it is important to give the other person the freedom to engage their implicit language, it is important for the listener to allow himself or herself the freedom to be implicitly present. All too often we overly safeguard our emotions by erecting barriers against them and we inhibit our own implicit psyche.

When we are sufficiently comfortable in the process of listening, we allow ourselves the freedom to interact on the implicit level. Once when I was in serious conversation with a young woman who had lost her son to suicide there were no words that I could fathom to help relieve the suffering that I knew she was experiencing. Sometime later I was amazed when she told me that it was the way I put my hand on my heart as I was listening to her cries that meant more to her than I could imagine. This was my implicit or archetypal language engaged in an unconscious communication with her. The movement of my hand to my chest was fully outside of my conscious awareness, but it was readily perceived by her as an act of empathy. From the moment she perceived this action the paradigm of our communication was fundamentally changed. This simple act allows the body to engage in a reciprocal response that activates our deeper layers of emotion and evolves our conflicts and grief toward reconciliation. This also reminds me of Jason's sorrow, and how he ultimately transformed his grief into a life of deeper appreciation for all life. There is much to be learned when we are silent[322] enough to listen.

We must begin to open ourselves to others if we are to become the vessel that allows implicit emotion and grief to be freely expressed. Nothing is more distressful to me than when a patient or client tells me how their therapist never really listened to them, or how they simply volunteered makeshift remedies to complex emotions. When I unequivocally listen to you, and focus my attention on only you,[323] something very magical happens in our shared space. The vibrational link[324] between us becomes an invisible matrix that connects us in space and allows implicit dialogue to occur.

One of the most striking memories I have of Jason's sorrow is the way his body quivered and animated his emotion when he was talking about his experiences in Vietnam. Somehow, across the space between us, I almost felt as if I was there. By listening to his every word and allowing his body to pantomime whatever emotion couldn't be expressed, I found myself participating in his sorrow. This may be thought of as a kind of constructive *participation mystique*[325] to coin Jung's term as he applied it to analytical psychology. The difference, however, is that the listener consciously enters the sorrow of the other to fully participate in the other's grief.

This idea as I describe it is not a classical transference where the listener is unconsciously identifying with the other, but consciously engages the other to allow the full expression of implicit dialogue to occur. In the same way that Buber discusses how a soul always becomes ill in relation to another[326] I believe it is only possible for us to heal in relation to another. When we suffer, we suffer because of sorrow, and sorrow always reflects a turning away. We turn away from outward space and enter our inner space where we remove ourselves from the world around us.

At some point the listener comes along. Perhaps this is what Buber meant about *grace* being an essential element of unconditional relation.[327] By opening ourselves to another we create the space that is needed for the *healing spirit* to emerge. When we discuss the *healing spirit* in relation to its emergence in space, we must remember that what is beyond our sense perceptions, however intangible, is still real. When I encounter the *healing spirit* in dialogue there is a sense of the ineffable that is unmistaken. It brings a sense of understanding and wonder[328] to the discussion that breaks though the thicket of emotion and frees the implicit mind.

Heschel, the great Rabbinic theologian, once wrote about the prophet Micah telling us prophetically that God requires us to "… do justice and to love kindness and to walk humbly with God."[329] I don't think we do this much anymore, and perhaps this is one reason why so many people today feel alienated and deprived in our present world. When we are in dialogue with those who grieve, or those who are sick or suffering, we must turn our attention to them with great intention. This reminds me of the Judaic term *kavanah*. Kavanah is meant to convey a sense of insight and attentiveness that deepens our sense of the ineffable.[330] Heschel describes it as *attentiveness to God*.[331] I think this really captures the essence of what is required when we wish to help lessen the suffering of another who grieves. It is not enough to be there, and it certainly isn't enough to offer simple consolation. We must *love kindness*[332] enough to silently reflect on the suffering of the other. We become humbled by acknowledging that we all suffer, and that when we help another who suffers, we in turn help all of humanity.

I recently had a discussion with a young woman who had read an essay I wrote on The Healing Space. She told me how she felt that her work with underprivileged children could be facilitated by focusing on the space they occupied. This is the point. When we engage in interpersonal dialogue we must engage outward space with the attentiveness of kavanah. We must direct our attention to the other as if the space we occupied was the sacred ground of the ineffable. This is what transforms outward space to extraordinary space and allows for the emergence of spirit.

Each encounter we have becomes an invitation to the *healing spirit*. Each morning when I go to work I recite a personal invocation to be present with every patient every time. I can always tell when I have been less attentive than I should have been because the spirit and sense of inner healing is never the same. The presence of healing, however ineffable, becomes an unmistakable experience to the focused mind. It is this attentiveness and focused intention that becomes the vehicle that creates an immediate feeling of empathy and presence. Once the other is brought into the space of interpersonal dialogue, and knows that he or she is unequivocally received, the deeper psyche will animate in both explicit and implicit dialogue.

When Jason grabbed his chest, and placed his hands on his abdomen, he was implicitly speaking volumes that could only occur when this subterranean connection of our deeper psyches was manifest. This is the vibrational link that is unmistakable when it is present.

It is the link that emerges when the only two people in the world that exist are the two people that are talking to each other. I see only the person before me, and I free myself of all other preoccupations. This is what sets the stage for the feeling that the other is being fully received and encountered. It is this duality of two persons becoming a symbiosis in outward space that is transformative. Sometimes the best therapy is to look past the labels that are unfairly put on people, and to simply give them a chance to implicitly express what they can't verbally communicate.

There is so much that can be transformed when a person feels they have been understood. I have often seen patients in emotional crises slowly evolve over the course of a conversation when they simply needed to hear themselves speak. They needed to move their body or sometimes gyrate a posture or grimace to express more deeply seated emotions. This is not meant to imply that deep seated psychiatric concerns are not properly managed on a medical model, but that each person has some other who is the vessel that receives them. The healing spirit emerges from the space within each of us.

When serious dialogue is engaged between two people, and the listener consciously becomes a vessel of unconditional presence[333] there is always a transformative moment in the dialogue. It is that moment when each person becomes aware that something innate and implicit has occurred. It is the moment of realization. Nothing more has happened that could account for the transformation and reconciliation of inner conflict other than the open vessel of dialogue. I have often been asked to explicate the method or the technique on how to engage or practice archetypal or implicit language. A colleague of mine once asked me to write a protocol that he could use when he was interviewing patients to enhance their clinical experience. The nature of my approach in deepening a clinical encounter, or engaging in serious discussion, is to engage a deeper *implicit dialogue*. You must become the vessel that unconditionally receives the other. You allow spirit to emerge alongside your deeper more implicit[334] language. It is the "I-Thou" relationship of Buber[335] and it rests upon the foundation of Judeo-Christian principles.

CHAPTER 6

IN THE SPACE BETWEEN THE WORDS

There is a spiritual landscape within our midst when we encounter each other. When we deeply engage one another, an intangible link emerges, and becomes an invisible fabric that connects us. This invisible landscape has been the subject of many theoretical insights in the world of quantum physics and is often discussed as expanding dimensions of reality. Is Jesus' oft- cited reference to the Kingdom of Heaven being in our midst closer to the truth than we know? All the great mystics of the world have always tended to navigate in this arena to the exclusion of a life overly invested in the material world. I have found that there is something very special about this apparent "betweenness"[336] that exits when we deeply engage each other. This landscape is much more than ordinary space. It is a transformative space that becomes transformative when we fully encounter each other in a meaningful way. To the ordinary observer, there will be very little significance to what lies within our midst when we engage each other. However, to those who journey beyond ordinary conversation with those who grieve and lament, you know that the experience deepens in ways that are not often tangible.

I recently had occasion to talk with a middle-aged woman who was diagnosed with a terminal form of cancer. As we sat across from each other there came a period during our conversation when she suddenly began to change her manner of speaking. There was a short silence that emanated between her words, and then an occasional sigh followed by an almost poetic journey into her childhood. Her words took on a liberating quality that almost felt like she was somehow creating space between her words, and this space seemed to create space between us. As I sat and listened to her, there were times when she almost seemed to unconsciously grope with the space between us, but she was doing it in a transformative way. She would suddenly stop her conversation, and then with penetrating eyes that engaged me, the space between us would kaleidoscope and narrow, only to widen again when she started speaking. There was something very significant that was happening both between and within us the more deeply we engaged each other.

It was the feelings, I came to understand, and that was the invisible but tangible link to the person who shared this space with me. As I began to consciously recognize a space developing between her words, I also recognized this space as the spirit of our shared emotion. The space between her words became the bridge of our reciprocity.[337] There was a closure of the chasm that was bridged by the silence in the space between her words and her deep emotion. This link between feelings, space and emotion would soon become an experience that not only deepened her inner healing but opened avenues for further self-discovery and exploration. We embarked on a course that joined us in a deeply meaningful discourse that centered on both our life and the fragility of life in the space we shared. As I received her, she became the navigator who commandeered the ship through the dark murky waters of our collective emotions. It was only by allowing her to journey in her unchartered waters that I could become the vessel that received her. Each word that she spoke became an instrument of poetic expression as it changed from one octave to the next and then retreated into utter silence. Our silence became our experience of space. It was the silence that opened the chambers of our inner world and allowed outer space to become extraordinary space; space between words.

The space between her words became an expanse in the space between us. Her silence filled the chasm between us and became a bridge that connected us. The depth of her fear and the emotional depth of her longing to complete her life's work as a mother and wife translated into a silent discourse. There was great meaning to the silence between her words, and as our discussion continued, I realized that there was great meaning in the silence between mine. This is *archetypal or implicit dialogue*. It is a deepening of the appreciation of our unique and often clandestine interactions that are at the root of who we are. It is how we communicate when we can't find the words to express the pain and sorrow in our hearts, or when there simply aren't any words that adequately express our sorrow. Ordinary space becomes extraordinary space by the simple act of being. When I listen to someone convey their sorrow, and they stop their words to bow their head and reflect, I know we are in God's presence. Ordinary space is transformed, and it is the humility of our humanness that allows spirit to emerge.[338]

The tears of this woman became the *bread and wine of relation.* They filled the space between us and became our spiritual bridge. This is how we allow God to become present. When we so realize the depths of our sorrow that we can no longer find the words to express that sorrow, we find the presence of spirit. *"Eloi, Eloi, lama sabacthani?"* "My God, My God, why hast thou forsaken me?"[339] I think this is the fundamental reality. This is what Jesus had to fathom on the cross. When we reach the depths of our sorrow we realize only then the existence of God. When this woman bowed her head and reflected upon the depth of her sorrow, she found the presence of God both within and between us. I asked her about her faith. With the greatest humility she told me how she never asked God to intervene on her behalf but only that God give her the strength to endure her pain and suffering. During this discourse, however, were the many unspoken words in the space between the words she spoke.

I suddenly came to realize that the space between her words, the movements of her body, the quizzical expressions on her face, were the real messages that her words could not convey. We were engaging in an archetypal dialogue where our bodies became the vehicle of communication from somewhere in the depths of our DNA. The bowing of her head and momentary silent reflection depicted all her years of sorrow. My eyes fixated on her posture and that moment in time assumed eons of significance. There was something very special about the space between her words, and ultimately, I came to realize that there was something meaningful about the space between mine. The space became the pause that rested our mind and allowed our body to reflect on itself. It was our body that needed to speak. It was her cancer in her body that needed to speak. When I slowly began to realize just how meaningful this "space" had become, and I allowed the space between her words to find their expression, her body seemed to relax in ways I hadn't seen in her before. The strained and sorrowful expression on her face lifted and she began to smile, albeit cautiously, but she smiled in delightful ways.

Archetypal language finds its greatest expression in the space between our words. It is the silent interlude that helps nudge ordinary space into extraordinary space and allows *the invisible bread and wine of relation* to connect us. There is much to be gained in the silent reception of one person by another. When we become an open vessel for the reception of another we allow them the freedom to let their body as well as their mind unfold in meaningful ways. Sometimes we only need to be interested enough to become the vessel of reception for the other. We do not need any special credentials to want to listen to our friend or brother during a time of need. The vine of interconnectedness is always present for those who seek its presence. When I think of what it means to really become an open vessel to receive another, I conjure images of an attentive audience listening rapturously to a singer who hits just the right notes at just the right time. The singer embraces the audience by unfolding their entire being in the act of vocalizing all their emotion, and the audience in the spell of the vocalist freely embraces all that is being sung. It is no longer just words, syllables, or gyrations, but it is all those things expressed in extraordinary space. The invisible branches of the vine transcend ordinary space and connect us. They begin to make words less important than their silent interludes.

Once we begin to recognize the value of the silence, and the space between the words, we begin to recognize the implicit value of being. By learning to respect the silence and the space, we evolve a new language of communication. It is a language of deeper archaic meaning where both anima (female) and animus (male) archetypes within our deeper psyche find their spiritual expression. It is that part of our brain where the darkness prevails but seeks its expression in the light that emanates both within and between us.

This is the reason why the silence is so important. Without the space, and the silence to create the space, there is no betweenness.[340] When I retreat and allow the other to advance there is a freedom that conjures possibilities. It is the freedom to know that the other can express themselves in a now extraordinary space that heretofore was not present. The person advances from deep within their soul across the rooted vine that now connects them.

Sitting in the chair across from me I witnessed the emergence of this rooted vine. I saw this grieving woman begin to break the confines of her sorrow and reach across the chasm that was now rooting between us. Slowly and then suddenly, I witnessed her smile, and then her joy. Something happened between us along the branches of this invisible vine that I knew opened an avenue of hope. It was just one human being trying to be unconditionally present[341] for the other. I couldn't help but wonder how many opportunities we miss to help one another because of the clutter we allow between us. The clutter that I reference perhaps has more to do with what presides in our minds than what occupies our space. Unfortunately, our space is all too often cluttered by the countless gadgets that add to these neurotic preoccupations.

By watching this process unfold, I once again came to understand that there is great therapeutic value in *being* as opposed to *doing*. Perhaps we often try to do too much when what we really need to do is open ourselves in a silent regard for the other person. It is this compassion and empathy across the chasm that allows the rooted vine to emerge and connect us. It allows our deeper psyche, if not our soul, to emerge from within us, and then to dance across the chasm we have bridged. This is the healing spirit. It is the spirit that was showered down from above implanting the grace of God within each of us.

CHAPTER 7

DISCOVERING OUR INNER SPIRIT

All through the age's mankind has always sought to define the existence of our inner spirit. Most everyone in the present day is familiar with most of the meditative traditions and have either tried one in formal classes or have just meditated on their own. In discussing *the healing spirit* this topic takes on much greater significance. Its' significance presides in knowing that if a healing spirit does in fact exist than there is great opportunity for us to conjure this spirit in ways that we may have neglected. Most of us, I am sure, have had personal experiences where we have had feelings associated with spiritual healing, but we have been left unconvinced. Then there are those whose experiences have been so overwhelming that they just knew that something out of the mundane had occurred. I remember once how a patient of mine told me how she just knew that all the prayers that were being offered for her had been the decisive factor in her healing. These stories have been conveyed to me over the years in the simplest cases of common aches and pains to the most dramatic recoveries from cancers that were theoretically incurable.

Interestingly, every patient that recovered from the more dramatic incurable diseases was always left with a resonant feeling that this spiritual process or presence was a more permanent part of their being. This discourse is not meant in any way to imply that any spiritual process or presence should ever replace the concurrent practice of established medicine but is an investigation into the spiritual process of healing in our individual lives. This investigation into *the healing spirit* obviously has a firm foundation in all the established religions, but we can also find many eastern traditions that commonly employ daily exercises and meditations in this regard. One of the things I have personally found interesting about this topic is that our bodies have a natural reorganizing drive that is always seeking its set point back to homeostasis. In my previous writings, I have often used the term "central reorganizing drive"[342] to depict the natural movement of the body back to its point of balance. This movement back to homeostasis is built into our nervous system by our genome and is continually working to keep us free from stress and disease.

Our topic, however, is investigating what happens to us when all the homeostatic mechanisms begin to fail, and we somehow discover that there is some force within us that offers us a glimmer of hope in otherwise hopeless circumstances. As I am writing this paragraph I am conjuring so many patients I have had who have conveyed stories about the emergence of spirit during the worst of their illnesses. They often told of how this *spirit* somehow created some glimmer of hope in them, or how they just knew they were going to be okay. Some of them prayed to a saint like Saint Anthony, or to the Blessed Mother, or to Padre Pio or Jesus, but they all had the same experience. Something had fundamentally changed in their lives that made them better, and even for those who did not undergo a cure or complete recovery, their lives were transformed in pivotal ways. There have been others who meditated and visualized any number of mechanisms that depicted a stimulated immune system like *Pac Men* eating up their cancer or infection. In all these cases, however, there was always something more than what they were doing that they felt was instrumental in their healing. It was *spirit*. Spirit in the form of a healing spirit, and most of the time in each of these patients, there was some fundamental belief in a deity.

Each of us has a healing spirit. There is no question that the human body, as well as the body of any living creature, has a built-in genetic blueprint for healing. It is the very mechanism that is always at work keeping us alive daily. In its simplest design, it is the cut on our hand that closes, the virus that runs its' course and is eradicated by our white blood cells, or the fracture of a bone that spontaneously begins calcifying and mending. Through all this there is healing, but there is also something much more than this. There is a dimension in each of us in relation to healing that is outside the parameters of homeostasis. I like to think of homeostasis as the continuous movement of our body back to its set point. It's like a rheostat that is constantly monitoring the level of a current, but simultaneously modifying its intensity to bring it back to normal. I think we would all agree, however, that in each of us there is something that transcends what we would commonly refer to as homeostasis.

Each of us at one time or another has had the experience of intuitively knowing that there is *something* within each us that is greater than us. If we return to the Judeo-Christian tradition this is the spirit of God in each of us. It begins as the Shekinah[343] falling like rain from the sky and presiding within each us as the divine spark and spirit of life. It is the "kingdom of God within us"[344] that heralded from the prophetic voices of old crying out to anyone who would listen. We find in Ezekiel that same voice telling of God's voice to His chosen humanity, "I will put my Spirit within you and cause you to walk in my ways."[345] This intuitive presence, in my opinion, is the spirit of God that is our healing spirit. It is this spirit in each of us that dwells within the deepest recesses of our being. We will not find it in any one facet of our body or mind because it is a dimension of our body and mind. The spirit in each of us is our "comforter that abides with us forever."[346] This presence of *spirit* is the healing spirit that healed the sick, gave sight to the blind, voice to the mute, and hearing to the deaf. The most important aspect of this healing spirit that seems apparent in all these instances, however, is *relation*.[347] Until I reach out across the chasm that separates us so that you and I are rooted together there is no opportunity for spirit to emerge. The greatest depth of healing occurs when the chasm that separates us is bridged, and the spirit within me is joined with the spirit in you.

We find the spirit within us by experiencing the spirit in others. When I reach out to you because I feel your suffering I open the hidden tabernacle that brings spirit to life. There is no greater gift that we give than when we freely feel the sorrow of another. There is great healing that occurs when the sorrow of another is freely accepted. This is what I mean when I discuss the *bread and wine of relation*. We reach out across the table where the gifts lie between us and we share the gifts. It is this act of freely accepting the sorrow of another that becomes the body and soul of relation.[348] This is the healing spirit.

In each of us there is what I refer to as a "psychic space."[349] In relation to spirit, I think of the psychic space as an inner tabernacle. It is the embodiment of inner spirit, both the Shekinah and the Comforter, a divine ember that only requires some other to ignite its emergence. When I have written about the psychic space in the past[350] I have referenced it in relation to the psychic boundaries that we develop from the time of our in-utero development. The in-utero child is at work and play exploring the boundaries of its environment, and with this exploration is the simultaneous development of an inner space. It is this inner space that embodies spirit. This space becomes the inner cell within which the child develops a sense of boundaries and safety from the world. It is the space where he or she will go to find spirit.

This inner cell is that space where all the great mystics have gone to find spirit and garner strength when the trials of life became too great. It is the internal domain of the yogi and the internal cell of the Jesuit who each find spirit and the Comforter in their own way. Spirit is within each of us, but it is my experience and belief that our inner spirit becomes our more powerful advocate when our spiritual energies unite with another. This is the bread and wine of relation. When I reach out to you and cross the chasm that separates us we become entwined in a reciprocity[351] that becomes the life of spirit. Spirit is everywhere. This is the fundamental meaning of "Shekinah" and is interpreted to mean "God's presence everywhere."[352]

In the orthodox Judaic tradition, however, it is not enough to know that spirit or the presence of God is everywhere. One must go further and directly bring one's attention to God.[353] This, I believe, is the fundamental reality underlying the *healing spirit*. We must create the matrix within which spirit is engendered when we encounter another who is grieved or suffering. When I encounter your sorrow, I encounter you, and I must freely encounter you as you are.[354] This opens the door and allows for the emergence of spirit. It becomes the matrix for the rooted vine that connects us.

The word *kavanah* in the Judaic tradition is the word that means to put one's heart in the direction of God.[355] This, in my opinion, is what creates the presence of spirit *between and within us*. It is kavanah that invites and invokes the healing spirit between and within us. Kavanah becomes the active participation of one's commitment to engender spirit and accept the emergence of spirit in the encounter. It is this component of fully participating in God's presence in the other that engenders God's presence in you.

Kavanah requires a fully embodied commitment to bring the healing presence of God to an encounter. The Jews of early rabbinic times taught that kavanah required a period of focused meditation before the state of kavanah could be achieved.[356] Perhaps we in our present society no longer have the focused attention necessary to bring spirit to an encounter, or perhaps we feel we are too busy to extend ourselves to this level of commitment. This is more reason why it is essential to reconsider our present course, and to decide if it is not time to return to a more theistic orientation to life and our encounters.

The healing spirit requires commitment. This commitment requires that one is fully willing to invest oneself in *relation*.[357] It is only when we turn to the other that we in effect turn to God. In the rabbinic tradition, this is *teshuvah*.[358] Teshuvah is a return to God or spirit and in the context of our present discussion it is a return to spirit in the other. When I turn to the other I must intentionally turn to the spirit in the other. This is what teshuvah means to me. Once the turning to the other has occurred I must now have the intensity[359] of thought toward the other and the other's spirit and this is kavanah.

Heschel discusses the essence of Judaism as the *reciprocity* within the relationship of God and humankind.[360] This reciprocity between God and the other is the very same reciprocity that we must seek between our self and the other when we are in relation. In my opinion, if we extrapolate from all I have said from Buber and Heschel, it is the turning to the other with the intensity of kavanah that creates the reciprocity that establishes this healing relationship. It is only when this triune of relation is established that I believe the presence of the healing spirit can be evoked. In effect, when we turn to the other we are engaging in teshuvah in the same way we turn to God because the spirit of God presides within. Our turning to the other is the first step in establishing the healing relationship but it is not enough. We must turn with our entire being to the other and do it with the intention of unconditionality[361] for the other.

The healing spirit is the presence of God within. It is the Holy Spirit of Jesus to the Christians, the Shekinah of the Zohar and the Kundalini of the Yogis. Regardless of the tradition or how a culture attempts to characterize spirit, it is God within each of us establishing a relationship with each of us. We must remember that God as spirit needs each of us to live in the world. Without each of us God has no place to preside in the world.[362] This is the essence of our reciprocity both with God, and with the other within which God presides. When I turn to you and for you with the intensity of kavanah, and with the sole intention of being present[363] for you, I establish a *healing space*. It is the healing space that engages the "between"[364] of reciprocity[365] and closes the chasm and creates the vibrational link[366] for the emergence of spirit that is the essence of healing. I think the hardest thing for people to do these days is to be present. When we engage another, we are often everywhere other than where we should be. I recently spoke with a woman who had lost her dearest friend, and she lamented to me how no one was able to comfort her because they simply didn't have the presence of mind to be there. They couldn't reach out for even one moment to be present in a way that would console her. It would have required nothing more than their unconditional presence.[367]

Perhaps the time has come to strip ourselves down to the naked essentials of relation and remove the clutter of preoccupation and the chatter of background noise. We have buried spirit under the clutter of gadgets and preoccupation and have lost the presence of mind that engages the spirit within us. When our society was an agriculturally based culture we lived in a very close relationship to the earth. Our soil[368] was our common ground, and our communities were predominantly neighborhoods of our extended family. When we met with each other we interacted in a way that made the earth under our feet our common link.

Our earth was predominantly the hallowed space that filled the "between."[369] I can remember as a boy working with my grandfather and uncles in our local produce market. Our life was difficult, but it was grounded on the soil upon which we trod and was centered by the church that stood as our symbol of relation. Everything revolved around the common ground of community with all its human hardships and imperfections. The authenticity of relation lies in our ability to fully embrace the other in all the other's humanness and imperfections.[370] This is how we embrace, deepen, and experience the *healing spirit*. When all is said and done we need to recognize that our healing spirit is the spirit that participates in the mundane as well as the exalted. It is the spirit that was borne in each of us as the divine spark of our creation and is the invisible force that brings life to each of us.

I remember talking to a man once who had a prejudiced view against African-American people. He professed being a Christian who regularly attended Sunday mass, but somehow had no difficulty reconciling his prejudice. He told me a story about how he once snubbed an older African-American man on the street who asked him for a quarter. I asked him if he would have done that if Jesus asked him. He instantly took offense to my question and told me how he would have complied immediately.

"Didn't you recognize Jesus in the man," I asked? He stared at me for a long time. The healing spirit is the spirit of God within us. When we turn to God in the other we open the gate that allows spirit to emerge and fill the chasm between us.[371] Spirit connects us and becomes the vibrational string[372] that allows relation and reciprocity to occur.[373] Once we understand the presence of spirit in the other our relation to the other undergoes a fundamental change. We see the other, but we also see beyond the other and recognize the spirit within. When I meet with another, especially in my clinical encounters, I try to focus our interaction in a way that links us across our common space. It is almost as if our words become a transcendent experience where emotion brings one to the realization of spirit.

I have recognized very early in my work the importance of the subtleties of relation. Every nuance, gesture, grimace and groan is an expression of an inner drive to convey something that might simply not have an equivalence in verbal language. When we become present[374] for the other we allow the evolution of implicit[375] dialogue to express all the hidden and transcendent meaning that our body may harbor, and our mind may not perceive. These archetypal energies will emerge in an unconscious *archetypal language* that will express spirit in new and transcendent ways. This becomes an experience of spirit as it is experienced between two people. We allow spirit to emerge in the between[376] and become a symbiotic link within us. This is how ordinary space becomes extraordinary space, and how the simple process of *being* is transformed into the emergence of spirit.

Each time we encounter each other we choose. Our interaction with the other is immediately recognized as one of ordinariness or need, and we choose accordingly. When we recognize need it is then that we engender, nurture, and embrace the spirit within. All we need to do is to silently accept the other as the other is and allow spirit to emerge. Spirit is the essence of the Divine spark within us. Its emergence becomes the transcendent presence that was best described by a patient of mine. "It's the angel in the room," she said, "There is no other way to explain it." This is how we encounter the Divine in our everyday life. God is both within us and between us[377] as the spirit of life and relation.

I have found that the healing spirit can be deepened in many ways when either person is seriously invested in the experience. Once a dialogue is established and one conversant becomes an active participant in fully encountering the other the process of unfolding begins. As the persons interact on the more transcendent level, there is an almost invisible pantomime that emerges. The dialogue may begin as a simple conversation with someone who is hurting or grieved but may then evolve to a release of repressed inner emotion. Once a compassionate demeanor is established the healing space emerges as an extraordinary space and links the other across the chasm. We become symbiotically connected by spirit that emerges first from within, and then across the chasm that closes in extraordinary space.

The transcendence[378] of spirit in extraordinary space is "the angel in the room." It is the experience of knowing that something more than ordinary has happened, and it leaves an unforgettable impression. It is like awakening from a dream, and somehow knowing that the dream was real in ways you can't describe. This is the embodiment of spirit. It is spirit across the chasm of time and space, and it links us across that same continuum once our unequivocal commitment to the other is established. When I am with a patient, or anyone who is troubled or grieved, I deplete myself of any thoughts or concerns that may interfere with having an empathic focused attention on the other. This has an immediate effect. On the one hand, it acknowledges the person, and on the other it confirms my commitment to the person. This begins to unfold relation. It is the embodiment of teshuvah, kavanah, and reciprocity as previously discussed. It transforms the simple and mundane to the extraordinary and divine. We can all become what is best described as the healing spirit.

CHAPTER 8

UNSPOKEN WORDS

I have often stated that unspoken words between two people are of much greater significance than the words that are spoken. There is a hidden language that is present whenever two people encounter each other in serious dialogue. This language may be present in general conversation between two or more people but my focus here is on the former. Although you may not know it this hidden language exists within the deepest layers of our brain and comprises all the subtle almost unforeseen movements of our eyes and facial nuances. Often, when two people encounter each other in conversations of sorrow or grief, they begin to engage each other with their eyes in very subtle ways. It is almost as if they are connecting some unforeseen dots on a matrix between them. These eye movements which may appear random at first have greater significance than you can imagine. Both individuals encounter each other, and before a word is spoken, they speak unspoken words. Their eyes dance in the space between them as they unconsciously express an emotional charge that has no verbal equivalent. There is space between their words, and the movements of their eyes fill the chasm between them conveying a hidden meaning that they both somehow understand.

There are regions within the deeper centers of our brain that maintain specific sequentially arranged codons that give meaning to the complex pattern of our facial expressions even before they are consciously understood or our words are articulated.[379,380] The implications of this fact are far reaching. Every time we encounter each other there is a hidden background pantomime in the deeper regions of our brain that are not directly under our conscious awareness. When someone is speaking to us the neurons within our inferior temporal cortex are already assigning a meaning to the words that are spoken even before we consciously interpret them.

When you hear spoken words, they are immediately transmitted from the inner ear to an area of the brain known as Wernicke's area. In Wernicke's area, also in the temporal region, these words are processed into an understandable context of language.[381] As these words are processed in Wernicke's area, the inferior temporal cortex in our brain is simultaneously assigning meaning to the facial expressions that the speaker is engaging as they are speaking their words.[382]

As you can see, there is a vast complex infrastructure of neural net-working that is at work receiving, integrating and characterizing the words that we hear, and the mannerisms of the speaker when they are being spoken. Therefore, the *unspoken word* is often a more powerful expression of our thoughts and meaning than the words we speak. The in-utero baby is already at work developing these deeper neural patterns of speech and their latent meaning even before the capacity for speech is neurologically possible. The in-utero baby moves, kicks, grimaces and engages archetypal language in the earliest days of its life.[383] It begins to evolve a meaning to its unspoken words by developing a meaning to each movement of its body. Even during these earliest stages of development, the deeper regions of our brain are establishing their sequential alphabet that will later become an encyclopedia of codes. Each codon will alphabetize a meaning to each movement and gesture that will later become our internal unconscious reference to the meaning behind the words of others.[384,385]

Each time we speak it is as if there are two expressive languages at work. Often, when we are grieved and not even sure if we can express what is in our hearts, spirit is there. Our deeper psyche reverberates through circuits and channels within our brain and is moving, molding, modeling, and bringing unforeseen meaning to our words and the words that we hear. The lines between spirit and psyche often become blurred as the expression of our language deepens, and we find ourselves seeking words that simply don't convey the meaning that we seek. But spirit is always there. It is the force that generates our movements and creates the space between our words. It is the pauses, silences, gestures and sighs that somehow help make us who we are. All of these become a composite portrait of our life between the spoken words. When I encounter you, I do so knowing that

I will bring all of these things to us in the dialogue that we create. By being fully aware and fully conscious of our relation I allow spirit[386] to emerge. I give spirit the freedom to create space over the matrix that may separate and confine us and allow our meaning to emerge in extraordinary space. The healing spirit seeks us. It seeks to flow over the matrix between us and transform ordinary space into extraordinary space. This is spirit in the "between."[387]

Spirit, psyche and God need to be considered a trinity of the healing spirit within us. We deepen the healing spirit both within and between us by first recognizing our reciprocity with God.[388] Once we understand that it is God who seeks us, and desires and needs to be with us,[389] we can then begin to appreciate the power of the transformative healing spirit we each possess. The healing spirit within us becomes most alive when it can cross the bridge between us and close the chasm that separates us.[390] The spirit in me needs the spirit in you. In the same way that Christianity recognized Christ's Holy Spirit as the Comforter in each of us, Judaism recognized and established the importance of God's reciprocity in relation to us.[391] We see in these relationships the fundamental essence of the healing spirit both between and within us. By finding God within us we find spirit between us.[392] Spirit becomes the healing force that moves the psyche and animates the soul and transforms the space that separates us into extraordinary space. We need to begin recognizing space as something very special. Space can become extraordinary; but only if we become active participants in the reciprocity that makes space extraordinary.

Until we recognize our inner spirit as part of the trinity of spirit, psyche and God, and recognize the reciprocity within that relationship, we are helpless to transcend ordinary dialogue into a dialogue of healing spirit. Our healing spirit is the spirit that transcends space and time and is incapable of being directly known. Like all archetypes of the soul it is only possible to glimpse at its reality, but we can experience the fullness of its presence. The healing spirit as I envision it is a manifestation of God's spirit within us. It is only when we establish our reciprocity with God[393] that we also establish our potential to bring God to dialogue.

This is how we deepen the healing spirit between and within us. When I am in serious dialogue with someone who is grieving, or is suffering, I must experience God within me before I can bring God to dialogue. When I try to live in this *reciprocity of spirit* I establish a covenant that I can then bring to others. Dialogue then becomes both the tangible and intangible expression of language. Tangibly you see dialogue in motion. The other moves, cries, bridges space with gesture, and speaks words that we hear. Intangibly there is space; space between our words, space between our gestures and there is space between us. Out of this *reciprocity of spirit* is the healing spirit that bridges itself across the dialogue. It emerges as the transformative element of spirit, psyche and God, and becomes the spirit that heals from within.

The greatest healing the world has ever recorded is the healing of the blind, the lame, the leprous and the bloodstained. He did this with glances and words, and love that reached out across the inner chasm of the sick. Jesus transformed ordinary space into extraordinary space. His words reflected His reciprocity with His Father, and the emergence of spirit from within. We can glimpse this magnificence, and if the spirit permits, we may even touch the fringe of the divine. We must become less if spirit is to become more. When we offer ourselves in sincere and humble dialogue to another we embrace the healing spirit. We create the atmosphere that invites the healing spirit to emerge from within, bridge the matrix of dialogue, and heal from within.

Life is the spirit. We must begin to reestablish our priority to more deeply understanding how important it is to talk to each other. Dialogue must become more than the simple expression of words. Again, I have found that the silence that embraces the space between our words is often of much greater significance than the words themselves. These unspoken words often carry an implicit expression of love that only our silence can convey. We must begin to trust spirit to emerge from within and animate our silent expression. This is one reason why our focused mindfulness is so important when we engage in serious dialogue. I must wholly *intend* to be present[394] for my presence to be meaningful. This is the *Kavanah* of Judaism. It is the act of willfully directing our whole being to God and living our life in a suitable manner.[395] This immediately sets the stage for meaningful dialogue and opens the space between us in meaningful ways. It creates the intention that fosters the dialogue that allows the other to be and feel received.

Each time we are mindful of *kavanah* we bring ourselves one step closer to mindful dialogue. This is what fosters the reciprocity of spirit within us and allows the healing spirit to emerge within and between us.[396] This is life in the spirit. We bring our practice of spirit into the life of spirit by directing our efforts to the other. At some point, we come to realize that the person on the other end of our dialogue is the ultimate spirit within. It is the Comforter or the Eternal Thou[397] that is the life in each of us, and the power that drives us to seek each other in dialogue. Our dialogue and the ordinary space that it occupies can become a transformative encounter between us. It can engender spirit and connect us across the chasm of time and space. Spirit presides in the space between our words in the same way that spirit presides within and between us.

CHAPTER 9

DEPTHS OF THE SOUL

When I was just four years old I had an experience of loss that became a pivotal event in my understanding of human sorrow. At the time, my mother was pregnant for what would have been the third of her two children following my younger sister. As you can imagine, our family and extended family were all busy preparing for what we all somehow knew would be my baby brother Joseph. Being of Italian heritage, our life revolved around this future arrival as preparations were made and the process of bonding was fast under way. My father prepared the baby's room with a fresh coat of blue paint as my mother dressed the crib with blankets and hung pictures on the wall. My job was to prepare to become Joseph's older brother.

I remember having had the feeling that I somehow knew this unborn baby all my life. It was a surreal experience that followed me everywhere I went and often became a part of my dreams. Joseph was real to me. He had a face and a personality and was a daily part of my life. I recall having had a dream once of the two of us playing in my backyard climbing on the wine barrels that my grandfather kept outside for future storage of the home-made wine we would make. We jumped from one wine barrel to the next like leap frogs jumping upon pods in a stream.

It was shortly after this one dream that I remember my mother going off to the hospital to have Joseph. She was nine months pregnant at the time and everything had gone exceptionally well. It was a sunny June day, and I remember playing in our backyard not far from the wine barrels that

Joseph and I played on in my dream. Later that afternoon as I was playing in our backyard, I saw my Aunt Madeline walking up our walkway toward my Aunt Nana who was watching me. She had a sad and sullen look on her face. It was a look that shook me to the depths of my soul. I instantly knew something was wrong and felt this overwhelming sadness in my chest.

"Mary lost the baby," she said. Those four words struck me like a ton of bricks. I don't remember anything immediately following my hearing those four words, but the grief and sorrow that followed would always be a part of our lives. Somehow, at just four years old, I knew there was much more to life than the ordinary trappings of the everyday. I knew there was a part of our inner being that transcended our ordinary life and perhaps was a gateway to spirit. The sorrow was something I felt in what I can only express as the depths of my soul.

The days that followed the passing of the baby were difficult. The baby had died in utero, and I recall hearing my mother tell my aunt that the doctor had baptized Joseph upon being delivered. It was a boy as we all knew. Unfortunately, his life in this world was not to be. I remember grieving not only for the loss of Joseph, but for the loss of not being the older brother and protector of this little child. It was a feeling that I would carry all my life in the depths of my soul. This experience would later become a pivotal factor in my understanding of human sorrow, and the importance of trying to understand another's grief. This is the underpinning of the *bread and wine of relation*. Human sorrow is the fabric upon which all the joys of life are weighed and experienced. It is the personal experience of loss that we bring to the table each time we encounter another who grieves. When we encounter another who grieves we encounter our collective suffering. We never grieve alone even when we grieve in solitude. Our grief is collective on the one hand and personal on the other.

At this very early age I learned that there was a fundamental difference between aloneness and loneliness. Aloneness was the experience of playing on the wine barrels with my imaginary brother before he was born, and loneliness was playing on those same wine barrels after he had passed. The loneliness was always associated with the despair of empty space. It is the empty space located in the depths of one's soul where only spirit presides but lies dormant under the grief of losing a loved one, and in turn losing a part of one's self. I recognized this grief early in my career when I was asked to counsel a mother who was losing her two year-old son to cancer. I could sense the inner empty space that extinguished the spirit within her, but I would also learn much later that this empty space could become the transformative extraordinary space of inner healing. Within the depths of our soul is spirit. It is the spirit of the divine spark that gives life and renewal when death and loss persist. It is divinity and the image that it conjures that can become the link to the divine, and the spirit of transformation.

Spirit emerges from within our inner soul, and as part of the divine spark it becomes part of *the healing space*. It is the imago dei or *imago Christi*[398] that emerges as the image of God from the depths of our soul and enters the healing space both within and between us. This, however, can be taken a step further. It is more evident to me now that the divine image that is within each of us is also the *Comforter*[399] who can preside in outward space. This, I believe, is how ordinary space becomes extraordinary space.

Recently, I was talking with a woman who had a terminal form of cancer. She was telling me how it was impossible for her to conjure thoughts and imagery that might in some way help her fight the cancer that was eating away at her. As our conversation developed, I asked her if she thought she could give her cancer to God in the space outside herself that I referred to as *the healing space*. I could see that this idea of a healing space outside herself intrigued her, so we discussed this idea a little further. I explained to her that I believed there was a healing space inside her that existed in a reciprocal relationship with outward space. This inner healing space, I explained, finds great expression when we encounter each other as we are encountering each other today. It was at this juncture in our conversation that I witnessed a remarkable calm come over her.

The healing space, I said, is that place inside you where the spirit of healing presides. You can let that spirit emerge in outward space, and maybe you can say a little prayer to relinquish the cancer to outward space unharmful to anyone. This idea resonated with her. I could see the color return to her face and tears swell in her eyes. At that moment, I knew I was experiencing the transformation of ordinary space becoming extraordinary. Her body animated, and she began to use the space between us in constructive ways. She gestured with her hands, molded space, and began expanding the closed circuit of her inner world to outward space.

This, I thought, is also how we bring *spirit* into the healing space when we are alone. It is the Comforter who presides within us but is everywhere at every moment. We unequivocally need some other to share our human grief, but it is through the gifts that this brings to us that the Comforter can emerge. The healing spirit becomes real in outward space as we leave the confines of our constricted inner world and allow spirit to emerge. We open our self and experience a loosening of the constricted boundaries that stifle and suffocate our spirit. It is then that we can see the image of God in transformative space as an extension of our inner soul. Perhaps we have lost sight of just how important the life of the soul is to inner healing. Perhaps we have evolved ourselves to a point where we can only find spirit in the nearest pill box. This is precisely why we cannot afford to neglect the life of our soul anymore. The greatest Biblical example of both human despair and human hope must be the agony, torture and crucifixion of Christ. There can be no greater example of prayerful introversion with the inner spirit of the Father than when Jesus prayed for the passing of the cup.[400] This was a transformation of inner spirit[401] in outward space. We find the imago dei or the divine image through introversion, but only after it is yoked into meaningful human expression.

The divine spark presides within us, but I believe it is in our earliest embryonic development as we begin to experiment with space and boundaries that we discover spirit. The sense of wonder of the newborn infant evolves in the experience of spirit found in the presence and coddling of the mother. This is the child's second experience with space following the in-utero exploration of space and boundaries. When we grieve and suffer we seek some other to help evoke in us the experience of spirit. Spirit is yoked into presence by the compassionate reception of another's suffering, and it is this experience that creates in the suffering person the capacity to turn to prayerful introversion and bring spirit to space and presence.[402] I think we can look at the Biblical example of the transfiguration of Christ[403] as an example of spirit emerging in extraordinary space. Through His prayerful introversion the presence of spirit illuminated outward space. Outside of its divine and mystical significance the presence of spirit emerged from within Christ, and in a transformation of ordinary space spirit was yoked into outward space.

The greatest gift we can give another person is the experience of spirit. When we suffer, we share the most human link to all our brothers and sisters who also suffer. We also share this common link with our animal co-habitants who suffer the cruelties of a world that often neglects their need for our love and compassion. When I am in serious dialogue with someone who is grieving, I share ordinary space with them. We sit diagonally across from each other, and we share our common space in a way that allows for meaningful self-expression. It is within this most fundamental element of human interaction that the presence of spirit[404] is evoked, and it is within this experience of spirit that later prayerful introversion can bring the healing spirit to a fuller presence for the suffering person.

Extraordinary space is the *presence of spirit*.[405] It exists in the difference between trivialities of conversation and deeply meaningful dialogue. This transformation of ordinary space takes place in the symbiosis of two human beings becoming an extension of the rooted vine and reaching out across the chasm that separates them. The emergence of extraordinary space creates a transformation of the person that can then evoke the presence of spirit through prayerful introversion.

Prayerful introversion is a long-held tradition in many of the religions of the world. We have all had the experience of turning within whenever we have needed to seek God or spiritual guidance. Prayerful introversion is a powerful human tool in helping us discover our spiritual roots and communicating with God in a way that makes us truly human. It is impossible to explain how powerful the *healing spirit* is until you have experienced it with another person who suffers. I can always tell when the spirit within the soul of another is emerging because the glow of the person is unmistakable. Whether it's the mother of the child who died, the mother of the boy who died from a heroin overdose, the Vietnam veteran, or the woman whose cancer was eating away at her, the glow of spirit is the same. Under the pain and agony there emerges a hidden smile that brightens their face and animates their soul; it is *the healing spirit*.

Every spirit is in search of a soul. It searches for that soul in some other who will open ordinary space and allow spirit to emerge out of the darkness. *Extraordinary space* emerges when the spirit in the soul of a person who suffers finds the spirit in the soul of a person who cares. Spirit then emerges in the space that separates them, and the chasm closes, and the healing begins. When we suffer, there is a darkness that embodies us. We are closed off from the world until our suffering is transformed in some meaningful way that allows us to ascend from the undercurrents of the despair. The spirit is in search of a soul. Like the Kundalini it ascends the ladder of our inner being from the depths of our body to the crown of our head; seeking, searching, enlightening. Then, when we encounter another who cares, spirit emerges and crosses the chasm that connects their souls in extraordinary space. Like the rooted vine, it crosses ordinary space and connects them as the transformation to extraordinary space takes place.

Spirit in each of us is always seeking some other. When I reach out to another the spirit in me undergoes the same transformation as the spirit in the other. By the willingness to give of oneself we establish a healing grace[406] that crosses the branches of the vine and connects us. It is an emergence and duality of spirit as the spirit in each of us seeks the spirit in the other. Once this relationship is formed, even in temporary measure, there is always a fundamental change that takes place in each of the two persons.

I have always noticed that each time I have established a relationship that I believe has evolved to a transformative level, I have felt the emergence of spirit. More interesting is that this feeling and emotional charge is obviously happening in the other whom I am reaching out to at the same time. A reciprocal dance across the vine of connectedness emerges as the body is freed and self-expression emerges in the space in-between.[407] It is this fundamental change in the inner self that creates the freedom of expression that returns the persons to the naked essentials of relation.

The *naked essentials of relation* are what I conceive as the symbiotic union of relation where self and other freely exchange across the vine. It reminisces of the symbiotic union in-utero where the embryo is in the safe confines of the amniotic cavity with relation established across the connection of the umbilical cord. This lifeline of connection is perhaps the embryo's first established psychological connection to its other, and in many ways, may very well be its last in the context of true reciprocity. When we engage each other in true humility we strip away the egocentricities that preclude the emergence of spirit. We slowly unlace the layers of egocentric barriers that separate us, and in so doing we invite the emergence of spirit. The *naked essentials of relation* become a stripping away of the pomp and regalia that commonly clothe our ordinary conversations. We show our true inner self to the other by simply being and invite the other to do the same if they feel safe and contained enough to do so.

This becomes a focused duality of two persons emerging in spirit and crossing the chasm. Then there is a fusion across the rooted vine. It emerges as an invisible symbiotic link to the spirit in one seeking the spirit in the other. In a sense, it is a retreat to the origins of relation when our innocence allowed our spirit to be freely alive in each of us. Like the in-utero baby engaging its amniotic barriers weaving a language of movement in space, we retreat to a spirit of innocence and reciprocity. Spirit emerges as innocence in the presence of humility.

Therefore, humility in our interaction with the other is so important. It establishes a safe reciprocity that melts away the barriers that separate us. I remember once when I worked in the emergency department of a large hospital in Atlanta when I had to confront a belligerent man from the mountains of Georgia. He was quite an intimidating fellow who stood about six feet two inches tall and weighed about two hundred and fifty pounds. He was intoxicated as was his ten-year-old son whom he was paradoxically teaching how to drink and hold his liquor. His wife was standing by his side trying to get him undressed for his examination, but he wasn't having any of it.

Finally, they called me in to help his wife after several emergency department aides had failed to get him undressed. I was an emergency department medical technician at the time, and when I walked into his suite I could smell the whiskey floating off his breath. I think this is when I really learned about what I would later call the *naked essentials of relation*. I simply walked over to the man and said, "Here, let me help you with that." I have to say it was like magic. His wife looked at me like "*you have to be kidding?*" He looked at his wife and said, "I like this fella."

This is what I mean by humility evoking spirit. Spirit that was able to cross the chasm between us and unite us across the rooted vine.

CHAPTER 10

PRAYERFUL INTROVERSION

In our quest to develop a deeper embrace of the healing spirit both between and within us, we need to establish an experience of spirit in our everyday lives. First and foremost, spirit presides within the inner sanctum of each of us. Spirit is the embodiment of divinity that dwells in the soul of every human being but needs the person within which God dwells to open the inner space necessary for its emergence. The naked essentials of being, of which I spoke earlier, comprises our ability to remove ourselves from the pomp and folly of the overly mundane, and engage the inner life of the soul that brings us to a higher expression of spirit.

When we are overly engaged in the business of everyday life we become further removed from spirit. We become deceived into thinking that our business equates with our value so that the busier we are the more valuable we are. There was a time in our society when God truly was the center of our world, and our life in the spirit became the basis of our life in the world. When we were a more agricultural civilization and were more closely bound to the earth, our doing was directly tied to our harvesting of the earth from which we gave thanksgiving to God.

God was the epicenter from which the earth and man revolved. God was the hub of existence, and like the spokes on the wheel, we were the offspring tending to God's creation. The spirit between and within us was ever near. However, there are great forces within the world that devalue our life in the spirit and cover our naked essentials with layers of superfluous activity. This is not meant to suggest that there are not mundane components of everyday life that are not essential, but we must reconsider how much of what we do each day has any real value.

The healing spirit requires us to develop life in the spirit. It requires a new and fresh orientation where our actions and deeds reflect God as the epicenter of our being. It requires a daily practice of inner retreat into meditative silence that will bring the experience of spirit to the soul of the person. Daily meditative practice is nothing new to the spiritually minded and has a long and valued history in all the religious traditions. If we are going to deepen our experience of spirit we must go to where spirit presides, and spirit presides within the soul of each of us.

We close our eyes and quiet the mundane world. We momentarily shut out the noise that assaults our senses and only focus on the darkness within us. Within the darkness there is the light of spirit. It is there in the depths, covered and buried under all the noise and chaos, but waiting to answer our invitation to emerge in us. In the quietness of our chosen room, or in the backseat of a moving car, the inner retreat is accessible. It begins to become our daily path, and the more often we make this inner retreat the better and more accessible it becomes. It isn't necessary to be an expert meditator or yogi to engage the inner spirit in what I refer to as *prayerful introversion*.

Prayerful introversion follows all the great monastic practices of prayerful meditation across the centuries of religious practice. One need only assume a quiet inner reflection that focuses on the presence of God. There are seated, standing and even walking practices of meditation that can be implemented in this regard. By taking a little time each day to simply turn to the spirit you allow the spirit to guide you in this practice.

One way to begin prayerful introversion is to simply take a little time each day in a quiet place where you are going to meditate for ten minutes. If a quiet place isn't available, you can do this anywhere that you are comfortable. In some traditions, the meditation is done with the eyes held open, so this is also something you can do if you are uncomfortable closing your eyes in the location available to you. The first step is to quiet yourself. I have found that breathing slowly into and out of the nose and following your breath as in most of the eastern traditions works very well. I like to follow my breath from the back of my abdomen then all the way up my spine and over my head until I breathe out, and then I watch my breath descend the front of my chest and into my abdomen.[408] This pattern follows an ancient Chinese practice often used in many eastern traditions.

This is a very quieting practice. Once you become comfortable with this ancient Chinese pattern, you can then begin to experience the deeper manifestations of spirit. This is where you begin to deepen your experience by focusing on spirit. One of the ways I like to explain focusing on spirit is by *intention*. It is through the intention and desire to experience spirit that we create the inner conditions from which spirit emerges. Some people who engage this practice will hold an inner image of Jesus or the Blessed Mother, or a favorite saint as their focused image. I have also found that there is great depth in the experience by simply focusing on the darkness and allowing your inner space to simply take on whatever dimension it expresses. It is at this domain that space and spirit become one.[409]

When I reach this point in the meditation this is when I will enact the component of prayer. This is what brings the experience of spirit into the domain of helping our brothers and sisters who suffer. A simple series of words that asks God to bring peace to those who suffer is all that is needed. The significance of this experience is that when we engage spirit within us we can then engage spirit between us.[410] This becomes the underlying basis of our experience. We begin to become more aware of spirit in our life by practicing the meditation that brings spirit to our awareness. God is omnipresent. God is everywhere all the time, but it is our responsibility to bring God to self-awareness. When we encounter God within us it is only then that we can encounter God between us. Spirit emerges from the depths of our soul only when we open our inner space. When we focus on the darkness, or the image or symbol, or follow the breath within us, we begin to transform ordinary space.

Spirit emerges from the depths, and it is we who can then bring spirit to outward space. In the same way that we focus in the meditation we focus on the other person across from us. We identify and feel their suffering, and spirit is there transforming ordinary space into extraordinary space. The dots on the matrix between you and the other are connected, and the experience of spirit becomes undeniable. This is how the healing spirit is deepened within and between us. This is also how I believe the healing spirit heals. Each time I have encountered another person in the context of the healing spirit there was always the feeling between us that something undeniably powerful had transpired. There was always some fundamental change in either our demeanor or our perception that eluded our ability to explain it. Perhaps the emergence of spirit is congruent with the emergence of our hidden background language. As we deepen our personal commitment to another we allow our background language to surface. This has always served as a signal to me that the deeper more archaic regions of my spirit, psyche, and soul were engaged.

Spirit emerges from within and crosses the matrix to the spirit of the other thus closing the chasm. Two separate and distinct worlds are symbiotically transformed into a unified extraordinary space that can only be described as *the healing space.* Space and spirit[411] become the unifying theme of inner healing, and I believe this healing can occur in both biological and psychological realms. I believe there is always a certain tenacity that becomes a prerequisite to the emergence of spirit in the healing space. It seems the deeper the problems, and the more serious the sicknesses, the greater the need for concentration in the spirit.

When I am with another who is suffering, I must completely remove myself from all the abstractions that preclude life in the spirit. If I am incapable of entering the inner world of this person, it is impossible to encounter them in the true spirit of healing. When I look at another and identify their sorrow my inner spirit must emerge from the depths of my sorrow for their suffering. This is what begins the healing process. Life in the spirit means that we live our life ready to enact spirit in our efforts to lessen the suffering of another. When we lessen the suffering of one we lessen the suffering of all.

When we identify another's pain and sorrow and it creates pain and sorrow in us, the depth of our feeling becomes the fuel that enlivens and energizes the healing spirit. We must remember that every time Jesus reached out to heal the sick He was moved by the depth of their sorrow. He felt what they felt, and then He crossed the chasm of space, and in the name of His Father He healed them. This should serve as a universal example to all of us who want to help lessen the suffering of others. Jesus instructed his apostles to go out and heal the sick in the same way that He healed the sick.[412] I think somewhere along the way we forgot our early lessons. We forgot that there is great power in just being there for another person or extending our hand to someone who simply needs us to listen. Each of us can do a little more. We can all start to create our healing space around us by seeking the healing spirit within us. By retreating within the solitude of our inner being we invite our spirit to emerge. It will enliven us and through its grace[413] will transform ordinary space.

If there is one prerequisite in all this that is the one necessary ingredient for the emergence of spirit it is probably faith. "Ye of little faith"[414] are probably four words that hold more hidden power than we could ever imagine. Faith is what gives intention its substance and drive. We create the space for the emergence of spirit by the faith we have in the spirit within us.

CHAPTER 11

THE CUP OF SUFFERING AND SORROW

I think one of the hardest issues that confront us as human beings is not only that we all suffer, but why we suffer. Human suffering and sorrow are the common plight of all of us, and no matter what measures we may take, life with all its potential hardships will eventually intervene. When I entered my internship and simultaneously worked at a nearby hospital some thirty-eight years ago, I made a commitment to try to understand the deeper implications of human suffering. One of the ways I pursued this was to listen attentively to patients who suffered from what would seem like mild or ordinary issues like chronic headaches or general aches and pains, to those issues that were life threatening like lung cancer.

What I found most interesting was that every patient always wanted to know "why." As a young practitioner, I was very quick to explain all the physiological reasons for either their headache, stomach pain or even their cancer or autoimmune disease, but this isn't what they were asking. *They wanted to know why they suffered*. I also wanted to know why they suffered. I remember one night when I was working in the emergency department, I had to start an IV on a frail ten-year-old girl who was a type I diabetic. Her arms were so thin, and her veins were so fragile that I didn't know if her veins could accommodate the insertion of the needle.

She looked at me with such soulful eyes. Her body was emaciated, and her skin was dehydrated, and just as I was about to insert the needle she said, "Don't miss," and then she smiled. Thankfully, I didn't miss, and I was given the honor at her request to always be the one to insert her IV's when she needed them. I went home that night and really labored under the weight of that experience. This little girl was so strong. I knew that she stayed strong to help her family who was always at her side. I could see the tears in the eyes of her mother at her bedside, and her father's gentle smile consoling her in the only way he knew how.

That night as I lie in bed I wondered, "if only this cup could pass from her."[415] The more I pondered this the more I came to realize that there was something extraordinary about this cup. There was something about this *cup of suffering and sorrow* that somehow fit into the general paradigm of life, and it fit in a way that was incomprehensible. It seemed to me at the time that this cup of suffering was somehow a necessary part of life's equation, but why her I asked myself? Surely, I could come up with all the genetic and biological reasons for her diabetes, but that wasn't getting to the philosophical explanation of why she suffered.

The way I looked at it was that she suffered innocently. Her suffering was independent of any of the obvious reasons for the depth of pain and sorrow that she endured. Her innocence only seemed to complicate the philosophical questions that I asked. Why did she need to endure this kind of sorrow at such a young age? Was there some factor in the overall paradigm of human life that I had not yet learned that would one day answer this universal question for me? Every day that I met with my patients I found myself asking these very same questions trying in earnest to better understand the underlying basis for human suffering. Each patient, it seemed, always explained their suffering as a story about their personal evolution toward some undefined objective in their life. Patients would make statements like, "I remember always feeling this way," or, "that pain behind my head was always there, but it's getting worse now." Then, of course, there is always the person who just knew when they woke up that morning that something ominous was going to happen like a fall, or the car accident that they had.

It was an evolution in what seemed like a drama that we all can relate to, but our experience is based on our own personal signature of the life into which we are born. Somehow it became obvious to me that suffering was a necessary part of the mystery of life. The *cup of human suffering and sorrow* is a cup of universal significance. It is the cup that holds our suffering until we reach that place of understanding when it can be emptied and relinquished. When Jesus grieved prostrate on the earth overwhelmed by the thought of his agony and crucifixion he asked that this cup pass from Him.[416] He recognized the universal significance of His evolution, and the life he was committed to live. At the height of His sorrow, and the peak of His despair, He abdicated the final decision to His Father; "only if it is your will."[417]

We are all committed to the life we live. It is a life into which we were born, and a road that we travel every day. The road is a tumultuous one with many winding paths and many unforeseen obstacles along the way. Our commitment to this path is a commitment to live our life fully and unconditionally, and to accept the *cup of suffering and sorrow* because it is a cup of divine significance. This cup is the *bread and wine of relation* because it is the universal link that connects us all to spirit. Somehow, to be one in the spirit we must be willing to drink from this cup of suffering and sorrow. Our hope, however, if that this divine cup holds the promise of life beyond our personal suffering.

This divine cup is not made of gold or silver or of any of the riches of our world. It is the cup of relation that offers us a *healing spirit* if we are willing to open ourselves to the fruits of its labor. The healing spirit is present within us as our link to God. When you suffer, and some other person sits across the space between you and receives your suffering, the healing spirit emerges. It is present within you as the spark of divinity as the ancient Jews believed, but it is also the cup of relation that heals the soul when one person unconditionally receives another[418] in their suffering.

The cup of relation is the cup of the humble soul. It is the wooden cup that holds the wine that becomes the bread and wine of relation. It is the cup that inconspicuously sits on the table between us but is present as the invisible link that connects us. I think there is a hidden message in the Last Supper of Christ. Jesus sat before His apostles as the humblest of men but did so as the Son of God. His cup was the cup of humanity's suffering that He would drink so that He could share in this cup between and among us. It is no mistake that this cup was passed from one to the other, because it represented our collective participation in the cup of suffering and sorrow. It is a cup that each of us will drink from all our lives, but it is also *the cup of healing and salvation*. This is the great polarity of human life, and in some way, gives some understanding to our human condition. In many ways suffering is redemptive. It allows us to enter our internal cell and introspect on the great adversities of our lives. We look within and peel back the layers that remove us from our inner spirit, and then allow spirit to emerge and expand our consciousness.

The many faces of suffering and sorrow sometimes make it difficult for us to sift through the mire of our pain. However, there is a *cup of healing and salvation* that presides within us ready to emerge from the muddy waters of our soul. It is the cup of the divine spirit within us that stands ready to help free us from our pain. Somehow in the basic paradigm of life, suffering is a composite reality that we all must endure. It is a necessary part of the overall evolution of our souls to ultimately be free and empowered in the spirit. It is impossible for us to ever reconcile the suffering of a little child, or the pain endured during a terminal illness, but the suffering somehow has value. It somehow fits into the overall equation. Our hope is that our suffering will one day free us from the pangs of sorrow and redeem us beyond our limited capacity to know why we suffer.

In our society, we are always running away from our suffering. Our lives revolve around the next pill or potion that will magically take away our pain or wash down our sorrow. We are consumed with maintaining our vitality and youth beyond our most reasonable expectations. Our hope is that we will ultimately eradicate our vulnerability to the natural evolution of our life, and in so doing avoid the vulnerability of facing our death. I remember as a young boy growing up in our extended family how differently we viewed our lives. We lived in an Italian neighborhood where everyone was related and worked together to insure our safety and well-being as a community. Life, work, aging, and ultimately sickness and death were all intertwined with the everyday joys that were a part of that natural evolution. Ultimately, I think this is where I came to know what I refer to as the *bread and wine of relation*.

Ritual, it seemed, was an invaluable part of the paradigm. There was always some symbol of salvation that was nearby whenever tragedy struck, or our lives became burdened by unforeseen events. My grandmother always had a statue of the Blessed Mother on her bureau with lesser statues of the angels and saints nearby. There was always some religious holiday that was being celebrated, and of course, there was always Sunday mass.

The crucifix was central in our lives. It was our hope that the suffering and death of Jesus would reconcile the suffering that everyone endures, and one day bring us to a better place. As I look back on many of the difficulties of that time, and there were many both within my family and our neighborhood, I can now see that each of these symbols and amulets became the *bread and wine of relation*. They were the cup that filled the space between us and closed the chasm of despair. I learned that the *cup of suffering and sorrow* was intimately linked to the *cup of healing and salvation*. They were the two sides of the same coin, but they were not opposite poles on the spectrum of life. They were both independent states of reality[419] that existed on the same string. This idea has profound implications because it underlies that there is a unity in all of life that includes each of us. The *cup of suffering and sorrow* and *the cup of healing and salvation* are a fused reality of life in the same way that good and evil are a fused reality.[420] We don't waver between the poles of good and evil but live in the reality of their existence. We stand on the string of this reality, and drink from each cup each day. Our salvation and our redemption preside in the bread and wine of relation. It is the body and soul of spirit and the unifying cup of life.

CHAPTER 12

TEACHINGS OF THE MONK

In 1961 when I was eight years old the traditions of the east were just beginning to make their way to America. It was an exciting time for those of us in my neighborhood who were interested in the martial arts because now there were books at the local library, and local schools began opening throughout the Jersey area. Most of the local schools, although just a town or two from my home, were still not accessible due to their perceived distance and their cost. Luckily for me, one of my neighbor's nephew was an avid judo practitioner, and a couple of years later he started a local judo school.

Always being the more serious-minded of my friends and cousins, I couldn't get enough of the philosophical origins and precepts of the martial arts. My childhood martial arts instructor, Mike, was the perfect teacher for anyone who was interested. With his long black hair and full-length beard, he exuded all the qualities of a teaching monk of the martial arts. His classes at the local Boy's Club always began and ended with a silent meditation that followed an exhaustive training session, and then there was the sweeping of the dojo floor; a practice I thoroughly enjoyed. I found this practice humbling like my reference to the naked essentials of relation.

Mike taught us that a clear and focused mind was always the first step in developing the equanimity of the monk. His training focused on long trials of repetitive techniques, and in the summer, we would often train for two or three hours in a single room that had only two windows and no air conditioning. These were the naked essentials that became a component part of our psyche. He taught us the value of simplicity in maintaining a calm mind, and like Gichen Funakoshi, the Father of Karate, he stressed that there was no first attack that was ever justified.

As Mike progressed in his own training he was finally awarded the coveted black belt of all accomplished practitioners. This was as much an accomplishment for us as it was for him because we would ultimately be the recipients of more advanced in-depth training. However, as time progressed, and Mike grew older, our dojo and the joy that it brought to us finally ended. There was a brief period when our Boy's Club dojo finally relocated to an actual school only four blocks from my home, but after a year the school closed and our training under Mike's tutelage came to an end.

To this day, I still maintain the basic practices that Mike taught, and when I think back to those early days of training, I can see how his early lessons had such a keen impact on my life and thinking. Mike was like the Buddhist monk whose humility and calm brought peace and calm to others. Through his early training, I was able to develop a disciplined mind and body and a helping attitude toward those in need. This is what our training represented to me. Those of us who were his practitioners developed the hero ideal, and like the masters from the ancient east, we were expected to defend the rights of others at any cost.

It was through Mike that I began to develop a more profound interest in eastern philosophy, and this ultimately led to my study of Buddhist principles in later years. In Buddhism, you are taught the very same principles that are the underpinning of the traditional martial arts. Buddha's first teaching of his *four noble truths* is basically that we are all born into a life of suffering.[421] For most people in western civilization this is a hard pill to swallow, but it doesn't take long to realize the truth in this teaching. Part of developing a calm and focused mind is coming to terms with the fact that we are destined to suffer. There isn't a living creature on the face of the earth that has ever escaped the inevitable consequences of being born into this world and that we suffer.

One of the most often asked questions of anyone who is confronted with grief and sorrow is, "why me?" If Buddha was asked this question I think he would reply, "Because we are all born into a life of suffering." This is a very helpful tool when listening to someone who is grieved or feeling that they committed some act that led to their grief and sorrow.

When we suffer, we are often overwhelmed with emotions that muddy the waters, and we look for answers to questions that are unanswerable. One of the first things we often do is to blame ourselves, but we are the victims of our basic human condition.

The Buddha's second teaching is that we are often the victim of our own desires in that we crave the things that we don't have, or we desire something that we do have to be dismissed.[422] This is another relevant teaching in relation to our grief and sorrow because we often lose sight of the gifts that we do have and tend to only see the scarcity or troubles in our lives. Once again, sometimes just giving someone the opportunity to explore their own emotions is enough to bring them to this realization. I have often counseled patients with terminal illnesses who slowly began to realize and appreciate the many gifts that they have in their lives. Scarcity often creates a vacuum within us that creates cravings that go beyond what we need.

Not very long ago I had noticed how my right arm was shaking every time I tried to use it. Slowly I came to realize that this wasn't getting any better, so I called a neurologist colleague of mine who agreed to see me. After examining me he looked me in the eye and said, "There's a small outside chance it's ALS." When he said those three letters I literally saw images of my family flash before my eyes. ALS would mean that in three years I would probably be dead. The prospect of dying in three years was formidable, but it wasn't as formidable as the thought of having to watch my family see me decline. Having to watch them suffer through my ordeal was something I couldn't fathom. After all, I was their guardian and protector, how could I possibly ask them to endure this trial?

The ironic part about this situation was that there was an alternative diagnosis that was thought to be less likely but also correctable. This problem could simply have been an osteoarthritic condition of my neck or cervical spine that was complicated by a congenitally narrow spinal canal. Unfortunately, the doctors really didn't believe that this was the case but decided to go ahead with a surgery that would at least correct that part of the problem. Following the surgery there was no way to know whether I had ALS or not without doing a biopsy which I refused to do. Due to the damage already done to my spinal cord it would take months following the surgery before I would see any improvement. This meant that each day I would have to live with the prospect that I still had this terminal illness, and that I would be dead within three years. Every symptom that

I experienced convinced me that I still had ALS and was still facing a three-year prognosis.

Finally, I began to take stock of myself. I started looking at my world differently and realized that there were little things I could do to begin to see the beauty and goodness around me. I was still in the middle of advanced Karate training at that time and began to reconsider what the principals of this training really implied. I began doing walking meditation on the grounds outside my home and prayed to God for the strength to remain optimistic during this time. My patients were wonderful and sent me prayers to patron saints like St. Anthony that they knew would see me through this ordeal. Each day I began to believe on a much deeper level that I would recover, but that lurking doubt always remained in the background of my mind.

My wife, Susan, was especially supportive of me, and told the neurosurgeon that he was wrong, and that I would recover. I began to see the Buddha's message very clearly. We are born into a life of suffering and we often only see the scarcity and crave what we don't have. Each step that I took on my walking meditations became a stepping stone to appreciating my life and the wonderful people in it. I began to listen to my footsteps as they trod upon the ground and marveled at the unrehearsed synchrony of the bird's singing to the steps that I took.

I also tried to remember the words of Jesus as I remembered them. "Father, if only this cup can pass from me, but only if it is your will."[423] I realized it was much easier to follow the ways of Jesus and Buddha and all the great teachings of the Judeo-Christian tradition when the test of faith wasn't so dear. I also learned, however, that there is a great deal of strength that can be garnered when we do have this faith. One of the most important things I discovered during this time was that sometimes you must simply let go of the craving for whatever it is you desire. In my case, it was to not have ALS, and to not have to suffer through the ordeal of watching my family suffer under my demise.

Each day became a practice session on the road to recovery. I slowly began to see that there were alternatives available to me on the path I was walking. Instead of craving health I began to focus on healing, and trying to accept whatever presented itself on the path I was walking. I realized that the process was in motion, and it was up to me to decide how I would behave during this time. There is a great deal of stress that can be eliminated when you simply begin to let go of trying so hard. Once you stop the craving you find that the path you're walking becomes less burdensome, and the obstacles along the way are reduced.

This is the beauty of the second law of the Buddha. Once we accept that we are largely responsible for ourselves, and often the cause of so much of our suffering, we then must decide how we are going to be responsible. This requires us to *act*. It is in the action that we take that determines who we are. By taking responsibility for our actions we make decisions that help us become better. We take stock of ourselves and assume responsibility for the path we walk. Life is the greatest teacher. It teaches us our strengths and our weaknesses, but also tests our spirit and becomes the ultimate judge of how we have performed. The Buddha's second law holds much promise in teaching us that what we often crave is to be relieved of a burden like ALS or cancer. In my case I was lucky enough to have a much less serious diagnosis of spinal stenosis that was eventually surgically corrected.

These issues are not so easily overcome. I work with many patients who have terminal forms of cancer, severe head trauma, multiple sclerosis and chronic pain. Sometimes it's very difficult to get past the fear of death and the physical decline along the way. That is where it becomes incumbent upon each of us to help *in the spirit*. That is when a deepening of the spirit will often bring the other to some level of reconciliation. This brings us to Buddha's third law. The third law teaches us that there is a way to lessen the suffering in our lives. It is predicated on our understanding that our suffering is in some way attached to our own cravings. We may crave to own a new car, be free of a problem or even a disease, or may crave a new or higher social status. All of this ultimately will lead to suffering. Perhaps the greatest form of suffering is the mental anguish that often accompanies our feelings of inadequacy, vulnerability, and pain. It is the kind of anguish that stifles the human spirit and preoccupies our mind with all the doubts and fears that comprise so much of our lives today.

The Buddha's fourth law tries to liberate us from this kind of suffering. The Buddha taught that if we saw the world as it is, and not as we imagine it to be, and we lived each day with the intention of following what he called his Eightfold Noble Path, we could in large measure eliminate much of our suffering. By thinking properly, meditating, speaking kindly, behaving morally, doing ethical work, concentrating on these laws, and intending to accomplish these objectives we could lessen our suffering.[424]

Although the Buddha didn't ascribe to any God or religion, I have found that for those who have a religious persuasion, and want to deepen their experience of spirit, the Eightfold Noble Path can enlighten one in this regard. I do not intend for this excerpt on the Buddha to serve as a comprehensive guide to Buddhism, but to instead serve as a whetting of the appetite to encourage the exploration of these principles. When I have worked with grieving and suffering patients, I have often used a meditative silence to allow for a lessening of the constraints that so often compromise a healing dialogue.

This *meditative silence* is a way to clear the mind and open what I have referred to as the psychic space[425] between the two persons in dialogue. Once again, the "psychic space" is the term I use to metaphorically depict the patient's inner psychic boundaries, and how those boundaries are projected in outward space. When two people sit in serious dialogue they engage each other within a boundary that establishes a safe space. This space reflects the boundaries of their inner psyche, and the distance[426] they create between each other is what I call the *spatial field of optimal interaction*.[427] This is where we define spirit.

Spirit is emergent from within, but it is not until we encounter each other that spirit encounters us. It is in this extraordinary space between us that we encounter spirit,[428] but only after we have experienced spirit within us. This is where we can learn from the teachings of the monk. *Meditative silence* is a process of unfolding. It allows us to unfold our dialogue in mindful presence, and slowly filter out the background noise that so often contaminates our relation. Mindfulness is the Buddha's meditative practice of being fully present and in the reality of the moment without letting extraneous thoughts interfere with our presence of mind.[429] This practice, I have found, fully allows the emergence of spirit because it focuses our mind in the moment. It brings the mind to the reality of the other person in a focused perception that sees only the other. This kaleidoscopes reality to a focused vision that slowly expands the psychic space and allows for the emergence of spirit.

The teachings of the monk allow for a quieting of the mind. I often think about our spirit as being shackled down by the constant chaos and background noise that rattles through our minds constantly. *Meditative silence* quiets the mind and frees the spirit. It opens the other's inner psychic space and broadens the spatial field so that outward space becomes transformative. It becomes the interactive extraordinary space where spirit deepens and finds its expression hovering in the in-between.[430] I have found that when you consciously focus on bringing yourself to meditative silence you automatically bring yourself to the *naked essentials of relation*. It is like a decompression where all the chaos and noise simply simmer down and then disappears. You enact meditative silence by first practicing and then doing. Learning any meditative technique that brings you to clarity and focus will give you all the tools you need to sit with another and listen. You let go of all the constraints within and around you, and simply allow spirit to deepen and then emerge. Meditation can be easily practiced any time of the day or night and does not have to be tied to any religious or philosophical beliefs. That is why I like the term *meditative silence* because it directs this practice specifically to the dialogue between oneself and another, however, its practice can bring great benefits to one's personal and professional life and well-being.

CHAPTER 13

THE MASTER AND THE DONKEY'S COLT

I think there are very few illustrations in human art or history that depict the virtue of humility better than Christ riding on the back of the donkey's colt.[431] There is no greater act of encountering someone than when we embrace them humbly. One of the biggest obstacles to our dialogue with another is our preoccupation with our own egocentricities. We forget how to be present because we center our focus on ourselves in often distracting ways. The Master and the donkey's colt are, in my opinion, a universal symbol of humility.

I remember walking through a local bookstore once and noticing a Buddhist text whose cover was of an old Buddhist monk riding on the back of a mule. He was a little stooped and garbed in an old dark Buddhist robe. The book was about implementing Buddhist principles in everyday life, but the more I thought about it, the book was more about "being" as opposed to "doing." There was something about that cover that was polarizing. It depicted what I believe is the naked truth of dialogue. To fully receive someone, we must become the empty container that allows that someone to be received.

We can only embrace another when we are sufficiently available to them in ways that are open and honest. Once I redirect my thoughts and concerns to issues outside the sphere of my encounter with you I have lost our connection. The "Master on the Donkey's Colt" is a symbol of transformation in much the same way as the mandala depicted by Jung in his psychology.[432] Jung's mandala is a symbol of integration that depicts an intrapsychic wholeness. This integration within the psyche requires a "letting go" of all the background noise and chatter and requires us to climb on the back of the colt. When I ride on the back of the colt I become integrated in the humility of our encounter. It is only then that I can fully embrace you because I willingly strip away the trappings of my ego. When Jesus lifted himself upon the colt he lifted his body and spirit to the body and spirit in each of us. This is the true essence of dialogue with another. It is the image of "The Master on the Colt" that serves as the embodiment of relation in the context of my meaning. This becomes the *bread and wine of relation* because it becomes the unifying experience that brings body and soul to one.

Christ on the colt is the embodiment of the divine spirit on the soil of mankind. It becomes an image that beckons our attention and should draw us to the humility of the Master as He rode upon the colt. When we encounter another in serious dialogue we need to stand upon the same soil. This is the symbol that should resonate how the divine spirit on the body of the lowly colt strode amidst the suffering crowd seeking the messiah's redemption. The antinomy in this relationship depicting the divinity of Christ, and the lowliness of the colt, should serve as our constant reminder of our place in relation. It is only through a real sense of humility that we can become the empty container to properly receive another. In a society where egocentricity predominates as a cultural norm it is often difficult to consider where humility can exist in our lives. Everything about our present-day culture focuses on our own achievements often at the expense of others who may be less fortunate.

When we ride on the donkey's colt we become part of a universal energy that is ancestral and archetypal in nature. It is an innate structure within our human psyche that renders us open and accessible to those who may simply need us to listen. When we encounter another, who grieves or suffers with any of the frailties of human life, we can engage this archetypal energy by simply being present. We can conjure the image of the Master on the colt and immediately enact the naked essentials of "being." When we conjure an image, we engage the image, and this in turn activates the behavior consistent with its essence. As the Master rode on the donkey's colt He became the naked essentials of relation. He didn't need to speak a word because the behavior generated by the image was enough to fill the souls who needed to receive Him. This is how we become universally linked to those who need our compassion and reception. When we enter that "psychic space" where we are free of our own preoccupations we allow our archetypal energies the freedom to emerge and openly help direct our behavior accordingly. It is only by willfully enacting the process that we begin to understand the degree to which we can reach out to another in need. It is important to remember that we all meet on a common soil, and it is our common soil that renders our humility accessible to us.

When we collectively stand upon our common soil we become the "naked essentials of relation." We encounter each other as part of a universal relationship that always requires one of us to want to receive the other. This is the prerequisite to becoming the empty container within which the other can empty their grief and sorrow. When we receive the other we receive them in their totality, and we open the vibrational link that connects us. This allows the open exchange of dialogue across the vibrational web between us and allows the *bread and wine of relation to emerge*. We connect across the chasm and receive the other in empty space that receives their grief and sorrow and then releases their grief and sorrow. Every time I encounter another who suffers it is the empty container of our relation that allows their grief and sorrow to spill in outward space. It initiates an inner reconciliation. The residues of their sorrow become part of the healing across the chasm of relation. In the other's sorrow, we identify our own human suffering, and this becomes the chord that orchestrates our reciprocity.[433] Once our connection is established in the space we occupy we then allow the process to unfold. We must trust in the universal energies that have existed before the origins of our ancient myths, and have come to us in our images, dreams and spiritual landscapes. This is where we often fall short. In our present society, we have become overly focused on our technologies, electronics, and scientific investigations to the exclusion of our innate unconscious mental capacities.

Our human psyche is a wellspring of unconscious empathy that is often locked in a prison of mental chatter and background noise. By calling upon the historical images and faculties that exist within the deeper recesses of our mind we can unlock this prison. Each day we need to make our human encounters a personal work in progress. We need to extend this to all living creatures and learn how not to pass judgement on the value of one life over another. This extends our empathy and our humility to all life in all its forms. Once we open ourselves in this way to all living creatures we walk the path of the Master on the donkey's colt. We trod upon our mutual soil and engage each other across the chasm between us.

Ultimately the choice is ours to make. We all suffer in the trials and challenges of our life, but it is this suffering that can become the path to helping those who also suffer. Once we begin the process of unfolding our relation to another we open the "psychic space" within and between us. The Master on the donkey's colt emerges in the chasm and becomes the bridge that connects us. It becomes the *bread and wine of relation* and the spirit of our embrace. Each time I work with a patient who is battling a more terminal cancer, it creates an awareness in me that transcends my immediate reality. I see this person in front of me in the spirit of embrace, and then recognize how the entire life of this person is brought to me in this relation. One woman who was suffering with a highly malignant cancer recently brought this home to me very clearly during one of our encounters. This patient's husband, her children, her pets and all her cherished relationships were somehow brought into focus. She suffers not only for herself, but for them as well.

It is this suffering that fills the space and calls forth the spirit of embrace. The encounter needs to cherish what she cherishes at that moment and allow it to emerge in whatever way it presents itself. All we need to do is listen, but to listen effectively we need to become the empty container first. This is what allows spirit[434] to emerge and become the link that connects us. If we think back to all those times in our life when someone was present for us we immediately recognize the special quality of the moment. It's almost as if time slowly disappeared in a moment of quiet reflection. Space and time became a kaleidoscope of mutual "being." When we fully engage our encounter with another we relinquish our ties to our self-imposed limitations. We become the empty container because we empty our container for the other. The "psychic space" within us becomes the space that expands between us and meets the other in their sorrow.

There is much healing that occurs within the inner spiritual space of the person who grieves when they are openly received. Their albatross of grief is lifted as the burdens of their cross are shared in equal measure. They become lighter as their burdens diminish under the help of the shoulder that helps them carry their cross. These are the universal lessons that beckon us. They cry out from all those who need to be heard because they grieve. All our burdens can be lightened when we share the burdens that we endure. If we are born into a life of suffering as the Buddhists say, then we must take responsibility to lessen our burdens along the way. There is no better way to lessen our burdens than to share our collective suffering by opening ourselves to the other. Each dot on the fabric of the vibrational link between us becomes an invisible platform upon which we rest our suffering.

We feel lighter because we have unburdened ourselves in relation to the other who is before us, and who has willingly accepted us in our grief and sorrow. This again is the *bread and wine of relation*. It is the path that allows our inner "psychic space" to expand the inner boundaries of our soul and meet the other on the bridge that now becomes the connection between us. Each time we take the responsibility to open ourselves to someone who is suffering we open ourselves to all of humanity. We participate in the collective sharing of our human plight and acknowledge our need to share the space we collectively occupy. Our space becomes our reciprocal domain where we consciously meet, and then unconsciously encounter each other. We allow our deeper archetypal energies to emerge out of the sea of our unconscious and guide us to greater self-expression.

We ride upon the donkey's colt and encounter each other on the soil of the Master.

CHAPTER 14

THE ECLIPSE OF THE SOUL

Every time I meet with someone in the throes of grief and sorrow the question of God invariably arises. As I think back over my thirty-eight years in clinical practice, I can't help but recall the countless hours spent listening to the sobs and sorrows of distraught and grieving patients. So many have gone before me as I sat and listened in my office, and often silently despaired over the depth of their sorrow and pain. Early on in my career there was the mother of the two-year-old baby dying of cancer, the mother who tragically lost her teenage son to a heroin overdose, a young husband whose wife was terminally diagnosed with advanced ovarian cancer, and a young woman who was date raped on a railroad track just outside her hometown.

Each of these beautiful people was suspended in the darkness of their soul. Somewhere deeply within themselves they struggled to find some glimmer of hope, and a source of redemption that might somehow save the life that was slipping away from them. Unfortunately, most of the encounters with these patients involved a more tortuous journey. It would be a journey characterized by hand wringing, tears and despair instead of the miraculous recoveries for which we all had silently hoped and prayed. Many of these encounters would seemingly go on forever. I remember one night after a long day at the office when I met with the family and friends of the mother whose baby was diagnosed with a terminal cancer. It was already eight at night when we finally met in the conference room, and before all was said and done, and everybody present had a chance to lament their sorrow, it was eleven. The heartfelt pain during these encounters was often overwhelming. "How could God let this happen," we all wondered? Where was God in our time of need? These questions ultimately became the impetus for my deep and philosophical inquiry into the ontological nature of God and our relationship to Him.

There is no greater ambiguity in relation to our understanding of God then the question of human suffering or the suffering of any living creature for that matter. Each time I met with this family the despair only seemed to worsen as the baby's prognosis kept taking a turn for the worse. At one point during our many encounters, the mother of this little baby began to cry inconsolably. She looked up at me, and as she cried she asked me if I thought God heard and felt her sorrow. At that moment as I looked at her all I could think to say was that I knew God cried as she cried, and that I knew God felt her sorrow as she felt her sorrow. This was the moment when I realized that all we could ever really expect from God during the best and worst of our times was that He be present with us during our time of need. It wasn't until this woman's sorrow became the impetus for my philosophical inquiry into these questions that I would later discover some important insights into these sufferings.

God suffers as we suffer.[435] When I first read Friedman's explanation of Buber's thoughts regarding God's place in man's suffering, I felt an over-whelming relief. My original feeling that God was present with us during our encounter, and that somehow, He suffered as I know this woman suffered, was consoling. This woman's agony eclipsed[436] her soul until all that was left for her was the presence of God. This is the *naked essentials of relation* the way I envision it. I came to understand during these encounters that it is God's presence that is the real miracle. When we suffer and become consumed by the darkness of tragedy we are stripped of the light that brings hope and love near to us. This is the great antinomy. God's presence[437] illumines the darkness of our soul and brings light and comfort to our sorrow. The immensity of God's presence extinguishes the darkness and secures our footing on the treacherous path of sorrow. This is the real miracle. It is the presence of God that becomes our comfort when our soul is eclipsed by sorrow. Perhaps the great tragedy of life is that we anticipate that life is without sorrow. This brings us back to the first noble truth of Buddhism which tells us that we are born into a life of suffering.

Once again, I think there is great meaning in the iconography within the Judeo-Christian religions that serves the purpose of bringing God's presence to us. This iconography, however, is as much a part of our human soul as it is a part of church symbolism. The spirit of God is within us, but our human frailties and sorrows often eclipse our soul and extinguish the presence of God.[438] This is the great challenge before us. When we encounter another who grieves it is only through our unconditional presence for the other that we can vivify the presence of God within them.[439] The presence of God within the soul of the sorrowful evokes the emancipation of their spirit to the space "in between."[440] When the other is fully and unconditionally received the chasm closes because spirit emerges from within and closes the chasm.

The greatest suffering occurs when we seek to cry out and there is no one present to receive our anguish. The presence of God and the light of His spirit requires another to hear, receive, and confirm that we suffer.[441] This is what opens the "psychic space" and allows spirit to emerge. When we encounter someone who grieves it is only by nakedly stripping away the barriers that separate us that we can open ourselves to their sorrow. This idea of the *naked essentials of relation* is compatible with Heschel's idea of piety as the inward turning to God or the Holy.[442] I think this really is the whole point of it all. Spirit is the embodiment of all that emanates from within us, and until we are ready to strip away the barriers that prevent God's presence from making itself known, we cannot experience the miracle that is *God's presence*.[443] For those who are willing to inwardly turn toward the spirit, and be present for another who grieves, you will discover spirit emerging and filling the chasm of pain and sorrow.

This is really all that we can ask. I believe that our sorrow is God's sorrow as He experiences the suffering of His children. The pangs of our pain resonate through the heavens, and it is only by our being present that we allow God to be present. God needs his human creation to fulfill Himself in the world because it is only through us that God can be acknowledged as God.[444] We must never forget that our suffering cannot procure divine interventions that lie outside the laws created by God because God is subject to His own laws.[445] This, however, does not mean that divine interventions are not possible because all things become possible in God.[446] This is our hope and salvation when we suffer.

When I am present for another who grieves, I must be willing to accept that all I can honestly do is to be present in ways that allow spirit to emerge. As the inward turning opens the gate, and allows spirit to emerge, it is then that the presence of God becomes manifest. This is the miracle, and it may be the miracle that allows other miracles of healing to occur within laws we do not yet know. The greatest gift we can give another is to unequivocally be present for them when they need us to hear, feel, and share their sorrow. This, of course, is no easy task. We must listen and open ourselves to the pain and sorrow of the other and allow our inner spirit to emerge.

Spirit emerges and fills the space that separates us, and then becomes the root that connects us. We sit in utter comprehension of the person before us, and silently acknowledge our hidden connectedness. This is the hidden thread that binds us and God and the events that brought us together.[447] It is virtually impossible not to consider this profound interconnectedness when we think about the myriad events that course through a person's life. Often, as I sit in session or simply listen to a person, and I hear their words of hurt, betrayal, and sorrow, I wonder about the paths we have traveled that somehow bought us together at that moment in time. There are moments when it almost seems mysteriously calculated like we were meant to be where we were at the time we were there. This, I guess, is the great mystery. It is that quantum leap into the world of spirit where spirit beckons us from within. It asks us only that we believe because it is only through faith that we open the door and allow spirit to emerge. When I sat in the conference room with the mother and friends of the dying baby, I can honestly say that there wasn't a person in that room that did not feel the spirit between and among us. It was almost as if we could touch "spirit" in the space between each of us. In the depth of our sorrow there was somehow hope and solace that within the connection between us there was God among us. There is no other way to explain the mystery or the depth of emotion that bound each of us. It was like a hidden thread ran across the room as we sat around the circular wooden table. It connected the dots and the dots connected us, and in that phenomenon, spirit emerged. In its essence, the mystery of human suffering is always tied to a search for its meaning.[448] We all want to know why we suffer, why we endure, and whether there is meaning to our pain and sorrow. Outside of having a personal faith in the unknowable God but knowing that the unknowable God is present when we are present for each other, may be all that we need.

I have found that there is great beauty in the mystery of relation, and that only in the mystery do we find the wonder and awe of spirit.

CHAPTER 15

IN THE SPIRIT OF HEALING

I have had many occasions over the past three or more decades to work with patients on many levels of both physical and psychological trauma. It was often difficult for me during the early years of my work to fathom the depth of human pain that I often encountered. In my earliest years, I had the privilege of receiving a personal letter from the eminent psychiatrist Elizabeth Kubler-Ross who happened to read a paper of mine which I believe was on "The Dying Child" and whom I was supposed to meet at a lecture in Canada. Unfortunately, I came down with pneumonia and our personal meeting never took place; something I regret to this day.

Somehow, I was always drawn to those patients whose problems, ill-nesses and sorrows were deeper and more profoundly complicated than the ordinary pangs of daily living. Perhaps my personal experience with the early loss of my sibling, and the sorrow I encountered during that time was what brought me to my patients. Whatever the reason, I always felt a deep-seated connection to the sorrows of the soul, and the depth of human emotion that it could engender. It was this deep-seated con-nection between me and my patients that over the years would unravel many of the mysteries of human healing. I came to realize that human healing required much more than what came from a pill or drug, and that it needed more than any one modality could ever hope to embellish. There was always something more that seemed to be going on in the background, and whatever that something was, it seemed to mobilize the innate forces of healing. It wasn't until many years later that one of my colleagues asked me to define this "something" so that it could be shared with others in the healing professions. Unfortunately, the answer they were seeking was not going to be found in some new technique, vitamin or drug, but already existed in the soul of the person seeking to help the other.

This is the innate gift of the human soul. Each one of us is in possession of the greatest gift we could ever give to one another. This gift is the gift of spirit. It is the embodiment of all those things that make us human and give us the capacity to feel what someone else is feeling. Each time I open myself to another I invite the soul of that person to enter my space and mingle in the life of my soul. I remove the barriers that separate us and allow the other to choose. The choice we make is one between encountering a deeper sense of self between us or retreating behind the barriers that separate us.

When I encounter another I also must make a choice. I of necessity must acknowledge the other, and I must accept them and the narrative of their story as they are at that moment. Their grief, sorrow, joys, and all their successes and failures become the battleground of interaction. This mingling of souls can only occur when an evolution of interpersonal relation takes place in a spirit of healing. It is this evolution between two persons as they open themselves to a mingling of their souls that allows the spirit of healing to occur. I have often been amazed at how powerful healing can be when one realizes that they have been unconditionally received in the spirit of healing.

When I encounter another who grieves or suffers it is at that moment of the encounter that I must become present.[449] It is in the nature of the encounter that my presence becomes the stirring force that inspires the evolution of spirit. It is not enough to simply be present in the ordinary sense of the word. One must become present with a unilateral focus on the other. This is what brings the mingling of energies to the space that separates us and begins to close the chasm between us. This spirit of healing is the spark of the divine within each of us.[450] It is the subtle flicker of light at the center of the grieving soul that patiently waits for another to help fuel and illumine its path to healing.

When the soul grieves, it embarks upon a treacherous journey. It enters the darkness of night like a wayward ship searching for the beacon of light that can bring it back on course to its rightful destination. Each of us as we encounter the other must become that beacon of light if we are to fulfill our place in the world. It is not enough to simply be a sounding board for another who grieves or simply needs to be heard. If we are meant to live in the image of the divine, then we are meant to be that beacon of light to whatever capacity we can. "I am the light of the world"[451] is the light that shines within each of us. When we open ourselves to another we allow that light to illuminate the world and bring the flame of hope to those who grieve.

Perhaps it is now time to stop thinking in terms of metaphor and fable when we discuss serious matters of the soul. It is all too easy to dismiss these undertakings as idealistic or other-worldly when these are the real matters that govern our existence. The choice we make when we decide to be present for the other is often the choice that decides the life and wellbeing of the other. We should no longer dismiss the life of our soul any more than we would dismiss our life in the world. Each time we meet we are given an opportunity to be present. We never really know when a grieving soul is before us, and this should always serve to remind us to be ever mindful of whom we are encountering. Our souls mingle in a spirit of healing, but only when the light within our souls illumines the space between us. Often, when I am with my patients in the treatment room, a patient may say something like, "I know you're busy, but I have one more question." I always take the time to tell them that when I am with them they are the only patient that exists at that moment in time. I think this really is the crux of the matter. When the door to the room closes, it is just the two of us in a face-to-face encounter. The space between us narrows and the focus is enriched to a meaningful I-thou relationship.[452] This is exactly what needs to be carried forth into the greater world. The relationship and dialogue between two people needs to be re-sanctified so that the divine spark within each of us becomes reignited.

Within each of us is the beacon of light that longs to illumine the path before us. It is the path that connects me with you when we meet and encounter each other in meaningful dialogue. I strip away the frivolities and see only you before me, and that illumines the space we embrace. Each of us has the divine spark of light that can brighten the space we share. When we unilaterally focus on the other the spark glows and our embrace is blessed in meaningful ways. For many of us it is almost impossible to fathom such a relationship in the presence of the myriad technological devices that inundate our minds. We have become the victims of electronic media to the degree that it has squelched our capacity to "see" each other.

To engage the *naked essentials of relation* we must be willing to strip away the trivialities of the mundane world and focus only on the other. This is the only path to meaningful dialogue and relation.

In the spirit of healing we must embrace the spirit within us and share this spirit in the space we occupy together. It is only when we openly encounter each other to the relinquishment of all other concerns that this becomes possible. It has been said that our eyes are the windows to our soul, and I wonder how often we look into the eyes of the other when we meet. This embrace is one of the most meaningful ways of establishing our human connection. We look at the other person in a way that opens the door to their soul and allows the spirit of healing to emerge. One of my patients once commented to me in session that she knew I was fully present because my eyes never left hers. It was meaningful to her because she knew that there was an unwritten code between us of unconditional presence.[453] It is this meaningful embrace that allows all the nuances and subtleties of human expression to emerge in the space we occupy and add flavor to all that we say.

Meaningful dialogue and meaningful relation are available to all of us. It is now more important than ever that we begin to focus on each other when we are encountered in meaningful dialogue. The space we share should become our communal line of relation that opens the door to the spirit of healing in each of us. When we encounter each other in this way the spirit of healing can take on manifestations beyond our psychological boundaries. I have seen patients so relieved and unburdened when they were unequivocally encountered in meaningful relation that physical complaints would often retreat to the background. Stressful headaches, abdominal upsets, nausea, back pain and myriad other ailments would become moot. This, of course, does not imply a substitute for appropriate medical care, but should encourage the value of meaningful relation.

At this juncture in our history we have lost our ability to communicate with one another. We need to once again feel the soil under our feet and realize that we are all connected in ways that supersede our technological attachments. We run the risk of losing our most cherished human quality, and that is the very quality that makes us human. Each of us needs to acknowledge that we may have become unconsciously hardened in our present evolutionary course. We have lost the ability to meet each other on the soil under our feet and see each other in relation. This is our greatest gift to each other. The *naked essentials of relation* are exactly what it implies.

We are present in totality and unequivocally focused on the person before us when they need us to be present.

It is impossible to know how many times we encounter those in need of simple reception because we are too preoccupied to fully encounter them. How often do we go to our doctors and health care providers only to be dismissed by a cell phone or computer? We need to re-think our priorities and take inventory of how far we have digressed from our basic human needs and traits. When we encounter each other, we should be enamored with a sense of mystery and anticipation. We should be drawn to the other because they have sought us out in meaningful discourse. This is what sanctifies the space that we share and allows the healing spirit to emerge. We have lost the sanctity of discourse because we relegate all discourse to the trivialities of the every day.

To engage the spirit of healing we must become a healing spirit. We do this by being mindful of the other when the other needs us to be present for them. It requires no more than our careful attention to the person before us in all their totality.

CHAPTER 16

THE MYSTERY IN THE SPACE BETWEEN US

Whenever I walk into a treatment room to see a patient I am filled with the same wonder and anticipation that I had when I encountered my first patient as an intern some forty years ago. My first patient was a little two-year-old boy who suffered with intractable ear infections, and his mother an R.N. who worked with me, wanted to try an alternative approach. I can still recall the excitement I felt when they walked into our clinic and I met him for the first time. There was something magical about that encounter. It was as if there was an aura that surrounded us in the space that we shared, and somehow that space was filled with mystery and awe. The most striking part of our encounter was how it seemed to kaleidoscope to a space where only he and I were present. There was mystery in this encounter and it was mystery that was filled with meaning.[454] This encounter became the pivotal event in what I would later recognize as the I-thou relationship.[455]

When I think back to that day what was most striking was the unequivocal bond that was struck between me and this little boy. It was as if I had known him all my life, and somehow, I knew that even before our encounter was over, something had already begun that would lead him on the path to healing. This had to be "grace"[456] in the space that we shared. I think there is something magical that happens when we are truly present for another. There is a mystery that unfolds between us that opens a spiritual door to uncharted territory. It is the territory where we can experience but not fully know the ineffable. This is the mystery[457] that illumines the journey and lights the space between us. Our space becomes removed from the greater world as our unequivocal presence isolates us in time and space.

There is great power in the mystery of the ineffable.[458] Perhaps we have lost our ability to believe in the sanctity of the mystery because we are too removed from the mystery to foster belief. We have far too many false prophets that have replaced meaningful human interaction with meaningless gadgets that take us away from each other. When I stand with you in the space that we share I stand with you knowing that there is an ineffable grace within and between us. It is that same ineffable grace that brought light to the prophets of old and created mystery in what was revealed.[459] That mystery is the spirit that animates the soul of dialogue and becomes the clandestine energy that animates the space we share.

If we can accept the mystery, we take the first step on the path that illumines the soul and brings life to the spirit. It is the path that can only be trod by walking the path with the humility of the Master riding on the donkey's colt. It is this humility that strips us to the *naked essentials of relation* and paves the way for the emergence of spirit. Until we realize that we can only bring spirit to others by humbling ourselves in the presence of spirit our task will always elude us. Each of us can engender spirit through humility and bring the experience of spirit to others. By practicing humility, we participate in the grace and sanctity of the ineffable and engender the space that brings spirit to life between and within us.

If there is one thing that I hope to convey in my writings on the healing space and the healing spirit it is that each of us can be mindful of another's sorrow. Our mindfulness can become a major motivating force in not only helping the grieving and displaced souls of our world but can contribute to physical healing in many diverse ways. When we are mindful we become fully present in ways that open psychological doors and tear down walls of inner oppression. We show the other that there is hope that they will be understood, and that their grief and sorrow will be received in the space that they occupy.

Our unconditional presence will encourage an expression of physical movement and psychological exchange that will animate in space. When we are fully present for another the chasm closes, and the bridge of relation allows spirit to emerge in the space we occupy. This initiates the process of inner healing. It is impossible to know how many souls are lost each day only because someone has failed to listen. How many stories do we hear about a person's sudden suicide or drug overdose, and all the signs that were present but went unseen or unheard? I don't think we fully appreciate how significant our "presence" really means to another in sorrow. Grief needs to be received. It needs to be heard, felt and encountered in physical space. The grieving other needs to physically move in space and animate their sorrow. They need to frown, wring their hands, lower their head and often sob silently so that their body can participate in their healing.

This archetypal language brings the entire self into the process of healing and helps to restore the innate balance needed to establish equilibrium in the outer world. We would do well to remember how far we have wandered from when we simply sat and talked and appreciated our time together. We must take the time to look at each other as opposed to looking at cell phones and replacing speech with texts. One of the greatest gifts God has given us is the gift of speech, and the second greatest gift is that it can be shared with another. We should not be so quick to neglect or disparage these gifts or forget the soil upon which we stand in relation to another.

When we meet, we need to fully embrace each other in the simple act of relation on the soil upon which we stand. This is our connection in space and grounds us in the act of relation. It doesn't matter where we are or what the occasion. Once we have engaged the niceties and social graces of conversation we then allow the other to be fully expressive in whatever fashion they need to be. This beckons the inner spirit by creating the unconditional atmosphere that opens the free movement of dialogue and engages the movement of spirit in the space between.[460] We can never truly know when another who stands before us needs to be received in this way. By simply becoming the kind of person who is responsive to the needs and feelings of others we evolve the dynamic of unconditional reception. We listen, engage the other, allow movement to occur, and encourage the emergence of spirit.

This is what needs to happen when we meet. If the other requires or asks nothing more than ordinary conversation then this can be enjoyed to the fullest, and with the same intensity and emotion. However, it is important to remember that there are many in need who are reluctant to risk rejection especially when the underlying issues are personal. By simply becoming the person who is responsive to others this assuages the other's fears of rejection and opens the "psychic space" to freedom of movement and expression. We all can become the person who becomes responsive to others.

One of the ways to begin the process of softening our sensitivities to others is through mindfulness. By focusing more intensely on the moment to moment activities and subtleties of our life we open ourselves to the feelings of others. All living beings suffer and sometimes by simply remembering this we conjure images that soften our hearts and make us more receptive to others. Each of us has a responsibility to each other. We all share the same space, and sometimes that space becomes crowded with extraneous clutter that prevents us from being present. This is all within the grasp of each of us, and we all have the capacity to mindfully open ourselves and create the presence that invites others into our space.

The space within each of us becomes the space we share when we open ourselves to each other. This creates movement and freedom of expression within the space we share and allows for the emergence of spirit. Spirit emanates from within and becomes the vine between us when we become unconditionally present for the other. Our mindful presence and selfless reception of the other is all that is needed for spirit to engage the space we share. I have found this mindful presence to be a powerful healing mechanism in all features of stress and illness and is easily implemented to compliment any therapeutic approach.

Sometimes it is helpful to recall our own sufferings when we are encountering another in serious dialogue or conversation. Remembering our own hurts and shortcomings can be a very effective way of humbling ourselves in the presence of another's suffering. When we do this, we engage the other on equal footing, and simply receive them in a caring and humble way. It is our humility in knowing our own vulnerabilities that becomes the cushion for the other to relinquish their suffering in the space we occupy. This release of repressed emotion and grief by the suffering other can be a very powerful instrument in their understanding of their emotions and feelings. The rooted vine is in the space we occupy, but only when the other and their sorrow are received unconditionally.

Spirit emerges from within, fills the space we occupy, and becomes the rooted vine that connects us only when the space within us broadens and spirit emerges. There is no better way to facilitate inner healing through mindful dialogue than enacting the *naked essentials of relation*. The willful stripping of all the frivolity, layer by layer, until only our humility and reception remains is the cornerstone of mindful dialogue.

I can only receive another to the degree that I am fully there with them. Until I can reach that space within myself and free the boundaries of my "psychic space," I am unable to accomplish this for another. It is the willful daily practice and exercise of mindful communication and dialogue that habituates movement in this direction. Each time I focus on the other I institute the process of allowing the other to engage me in a meaningful way. This allows us to take the first step in the many steps that will be taken to enact spirit in the space we share.

There will be no doubt in the minds of the persons engaged in this process that spirit both fills the soul and the space. The emotional discharge and release of pent up psychic energy settles into the space that is shared, and there is freedom of both dialogue and movement. There is much to be said for the simple way we once talked to each other in ordinary conversation. My fondest memories are of coming home from grade school on a Monday afternoon and visiting my grandmother. On Mondays, we had early dismissal, so the local public-school children could attend religious classes at our parochial school.

When I walked into the front door of her home, which adjoined a little grocery store we owned, there would be three or four of our aunts who came over from Italy sitting around the kitchen table. You could smell the aroma of home brewed percolated coffee the minute you walked into the hall. Everyone seemed to have something important to say, and it was always said in Italian. It was like an Italian festival of neighborhood women with no topic being too trivial or too serious to discuss. Everyone at the table all lived within a four-block radius of each other, and their conversations were a grounding in all the things that were important to them.

I learned much from listening and watching the old women. Each of them seemed to have a knack for sitting on their common soil and simply listening to each other. Their cups and saucers and the old pot of coffee were dots along the matrix that connected them in the space they shared. They would move their arms, raise their voice, sometimes shout in exuberant laughter, and sometimes cry about things I was too young to understand. There was no clutter, no frivolity, and no shame in their conversation as they simply listened and received each other.

Each of them in their own way became the empty container for the other. They were attentive to each other's stories and would often engage each other with a meaningful touch of the hand or warm embrace. I remember once as a little boy watching them interact and thinking how animated they were in their interactions. Often, they would laugh so hard about things I didn't completely understand that tears would stroll down their cheeks. Their conversations were meaningful because each one of them was genuinely interested in the other, and there were no preoccupations beyond the immediate concerns of their daily lives on the soil. Most of these women knew the hardships of daily life. They were women who were up at four in the morning working alongside their husbands until late at night. They had given birth to children, lost children, worked hard and paid bills. They fully understood human sorrow.

I could always tell when their conversations would turn to the more taciturn and serious matters of life. They would suddenly become more attentive almost as if there was a heaviness embodying them. Not fully understanding all their Italian I would look for signals in their mannerisms that would render some meaning to the seriousness of their conversation. Words that were previously stated in loud tones would suddenly soften as they cushioned the sorrowful tones of the other. Each of them was fully present. They were humble because humility was the path that they trod in life. They didn't need to practice humility because riding on the donkey's colt was the path they chose in life.

These are the lessons of the Master riding on the donkey's colt. These women embodied humility and empathy, and like the dots on the matrix that connected them, they were unified in a symbiosis of reciprocity. The mystery that exists between each of us is a mystery of the spirit within each of us. When we open ourselves to the other we open them to all the possibilities of life in the spirit. We invite them to participate in the spirit within us in the hope of bringing the spirit in them to life in the space we share.

CHAPTER 17

IN THE SPIRIT OF ENCOUNTER

W e are the architects of relation. By opening ourselves to the other we invite the emergence of spirit in the space between us. Spirit emerges from within and connects us in space, and it is spirit that frees the bonds of constraint that encumber us. The elderly Italian women of the neighborhood had a natural inclination in the spirit. Their humility and collective sorrows were never too far from the surface of their hearts. It was their sufferings and sorrows that became the bedrock of their empathy and receptivity for the other.

The mystery between us is in the mystery that exists between the spirit in me and the spirit in you. Within this mystery is where all the potential for inner healing presides. Jesus was always moved by His compassion for the sick and suffering. He was never too far removed from the sorrows of humankind to neglect the blind, the mute, the leprous and the lame. In the heart of Jesus is the suffering of all humankind, and it is this suffering which is the embodiment of empathy for all those who suffer.

Again, I think the iconography of religious history is a working mosaic for the humble soul. Perhaps this is why our older generations venerated the saints whose sufferings were always close to their hearts. Our ancestor's life was a life on the soil. It was the same soil where they built their homes, ran their businesses, raised their families, and prayed in their churches. We have lost so much in our quest to advance our technologies and ideologies that we have in large part lost our life in the spirit. Within the depths of our soul there is a hidden landscape that we have largely ignored. It is a vibrant living unconscious state of hidden potential that awaits awakening in the spirit. When I see you as my only other, it is at that moment in time and space that I awaken the spirit within us. It engenders the vibrational matrix between us and enables my devotion to your presence to connect us. In that moment there is healing. I believe we largely underestimate the healing energies of our collective soul. Within the deepest recesses of our soul there is an unconscious spirit that moves and animates us and awaits our beckoning. It represents our collective ancestral heritage and all the possibilities that life in the spirit has to offer.

There is a timeless spirit in our souls that spans the multiple generations that precede us. It is our life force and it can be accessed for either of two poles of our being. We don't have to look far to see how destructive the negative pole of our unconscious energy can be. Just a simple look at our wars, poverty, discrimination and homelessness is convincing. It is our choice. We decide how to awaken the spirit that gives us life. We need to understand that each time we encounter each other we choose. We are the agencies of movement. When I choose to encounter you in totality I activate a sequence of movements that beckons the spirit of healing within and between us. It evolves to an orchestrated pantomime where our spirits meet and dance in the space between us. We connect the dots on our invisible matrix and engage a dimension of ourselves that transcends our cognitive understanding. We encounter and behold the bread and wine of relation and deconstruct our barriers.

In every simple movement there is a grand counterpart. When I choose to be present for you I choose to be present for the world. We are a microcosm of the greater world which we inhabit and no one choice that we make can ever be separated from the rest of the world. When I encounter you in sacred space I make the world a more sacred place. I choose peace over war, charity over poverty, equality over discrimination and love over hatred and homelessness. This is the dimension to which we must see our choice when we encounter those in need or when we stand in open dialogue with another who needs to be heard. Each time we become present for the other we become present for everyone. This is the rippling wave of unconditionality.

When we encounter each other in meaningful dialogue our silence in the presence of the other becomes our mutual link. I allow the other to emerge in all their hidden potentialities and invoke the other's unconscious into meaningful expression. I abandon my need to interject, to lure, or to direct my thoughts. I listen to the one who needs to talk to me and I become present for the one who sits before me. I serve them as only I can in all my totality including all the imperfections that are a part of who I am.

Humility is best expressed in silence. It removes the veil that separates our spirit from the one who sits before us. Whenever we try to make ourselves more, spirit becomes less, and we become disconnected isolated egos. Each time I open myself to another I open the other to a world of possibilities. I allow the other to be present as I am present, and this engenders the emergence of the invisible matrix that connects us. It is the matrix that allows the spirit within us to emerge on the vine that connects us. It becomes a *healing spirit* hovering within a *healing space* across the rooted vine that embodies us.

The *naked essentials of relation* strip the ego of all its preoccupations that dampen unconditional presence. When I am sufficiently present for another I am in the spirit of relation on the matrix in the space between us. This, once again, becomes the bread and wine of our relation. We have taken the intangible and reconstructed space where our words, movements, grimaces and all those nuances that express our implicit being are connected along the invisible matrix. It is this implicit connection that becomes the link that captures us. It moves us beyond the ordinary and evolves to an extraordinary interrelationship that we share. There are many layers to the process of dialogue. One of the ways this was brought home to me is the experiences I have had in some of my work with autistic children. Often, the child will squirm, grimace, utter unintelligible syllables and gyrate in chaotic patterns of behavior. This behavior, however, is meaningful and depicts the child's inner psychic organization that is at work. It is almost as if the brain is trying to reestablish a new organizational set point from which it can better navigate the world. There is so much we can learn from these beautiful children who frantically try to connect the dots that help them make sense of their world. I have often found that they direct their movements to suit the psychic state that consumes them. One of the children I have worked with always tightly shut her eyes and squirmed on the treatment table in what I have described as the tadpole child.[461] These children will divert their eyes in spontaneous conjugate movements that will often seem to balance a body habitus that is asymmetrically moving in space. They are connecting the dots on the invisible matrix in the only way they can. It is their attempt at neural integration in a way that better defines the space that separates them from the world. This is their implicit language and when we engage them in the language they express the space that separates them now helps integrate them.

Another child I have worked with consistently moved her hands to her face and closed her eyes almost as if she was trying to shut out the world. When I encountered her, however, in a spatial field that suited her space she would relax her eyes and her hands would meet mine in space. Her body would relax, and she would become calm. It was almost as if she was repositioning the matrix in the space we occupied and connecting the dots in a way that made more sense. What was most noticeable was the way her darting conjugate eye movements stabilized and became more centered on me in the space we occupied. She would begin to center her eye gazes and her hands would meet mine in the space between us in a way that suggested a stable set point. Her fingers would intertwine around mine and she would hold my gaze. This is the spirit of encounter. Together we walked the path of the *healing space* and allowed the emergence of spirit to manifest in the space we occupied. Together we held the branches of the rooted vine in a way that connected us along the invisible matrix and experienced the presence of the *healing spirit*.

One of the facets of engaging the healing spirit is to recognize the implicit similarities in how people navigate the space they occupy. For instance, one of my patients who suffers with progressive multiple sclerosis and has serious ataxic gait abnormalities often navigates in ways like the autistic children that I see. Their nervous system disintegration although significantly different in pathophysiology alters the matrix in the space between them and their world. When we meet them unconditionally we make the invisible matrix that separates us a more tangible grid upon which they can grasp and connect. This is the *healing spirit* in the spirit of encounter. It helps create whatever contribution you make to the person before you a little better, a little more whole.

We should not underestimate the significance of our healing encounters. Whether we are a friend listening to a grieving other or a doctor in the throes of working with a terminally ill cancer patient the healing space is there. Each movement of the hands, gaze of the eyes or grimace of the face is connecting some dot on the matrix that brings us closer. It is movement toward symbiosis and union. It is the invisible matrix that connects and unites us in our common heritage of universal suffering. There is meaning in the space we occupy and that meaning is enhanced when we occupy that space together. It allows us to share our human burdens and find meaning in our suffering because we come to realize that suffering is what drives our quest for a meaningful life.

The Buddha said that we are born into a life of suffering. We are destined to suffer because we are born into a world that separates us and largely squashes the human spirit. Our salvation lies in the presence of spirit that can only be engendered when we open ourselves to each other in the space we occupy. I have heard countless stories from patients who have told me of their personal encounters with spirit. How in times of despair they could feel God's presence both within them and outside them as they grieved with some other. They could feel the matrix of their space thicken almost as if it was becoming a tangible connection they could see.

This is what constitutes the spirit of encounter. It occurs when we willfully enter the healing space and allow spirit to emerge in ways that connect us. If suffering is our human heritage, then our shared suffering along the matrix between us may be one way to help reduce our burdens. The rooted vine is within us and its branches seek to connect us in the spirit. When we grasp the branches between us we embrace the spirit within us and God is present. This is the healing spirit that fills our space and engenders life in the space we occupy.

CHAPTER 18

THE NEUROLOGY OF THE SPACE "IN-BETWEEN"

It is important to recognize that there are highly evolved biological pathways that make it possible for us to experience the conscious state. The moment we encounter each other our brain immediately activates specific neural pathways that create a cognitive impression of our experience. More important than this is the fact that all of this happens before our conscious awareness of the experience. When we encounter each other a part of our brain called the inferior temporal cortex immediately codes the complex patterns of our facial expressions.[462] If our facial expressions present any pattern that is analogous to even a subtle significant social cue our brain will process what we see long before we are consciously aware of it.[463] This is what makes the space "between I and You"[464] a space of integral relation. When I enter the space between us I enter a shared responsibility with you to be present. If I lack being present I negate you.

We now know that our brain has what is known as a *salience network*. The salience network comprises a paralimbic system centered in the anterior insula located deep within our brain near the front of our ear and the dorsal anterior cingulate cortex in the deep center of our brain. It further includes the amygdala, the ventral striatum, the substantia nigra and the ventral tegmental area[465] also located in the deep central part of our brain. We can think of the salience network as that part of our brain that prioritizes the incoming streams of information we receive and then directs our attention to what is deemed most important and in need of further analysis.

When we encounter each other in ordinary space the salience network immediately activates in multiple parallel circuits within our brain. It begins to prioritize all the nuances that we may or may not see and creates an interactive model that responds to what it perceives. The part of the salience network known as the striatum, which is two separate but interactive brain regions, is exquisitely sensitive to our vocalization of speech or even just the movement of our lips.[466] Our seemingly innocuous interactions are evaluated on the most remote level of our expression. When we encounter each other in ordinary space we embrace our interactive interconnected worlds in both conscious and unconscious spheres of relation. When I enter relation with you unconditionally I engage the spirit within you. My demeanor becomes an unconscious interactive stimulus that activates your salient reception. This lowers our defenses and opens the door to a greater freedom of expression. We open the psychic space through salience and allow the subtle transformation of ordinary space to become the extraordinary space "in-between."[467]

I think of the salience network as the garden within which the rooted vine is planted. As we nurture and care for the soil within us we grow the vine that will one day convey the spirit over the branches that connect us. This is how we transform ordinary space into extraordinary space. The space "in-between" becomes the invisible matrix that connects us as the spirit within us crosses the branches of the rooted vine and fills the space we occupy. The neural underpinnings of the space we share when we encounter each other has far reaching effects. In my clinical work I have studied the use of eye movements as a method to regulate neural conduction patterns that help restore dysfunctional states. It was this original work that heightened my observations of patients as I watched their many eye movements during our dialogue or sessions. Each patient seemed to move their eyes in ways that connected us along the invisible matrix between us. The more I studied this phenomenon the more I came to understand that these eye movements were connected to numerous neural circuits in the brain.

For instance, the movements of our eyes are a motive force in transmitting signals to the very centers of our brain that comprise the salience network.[468] Whenever we encounter one another we engage in a deeply unconscious pantomime that expresses a hidden language within which

I believe lies the essence of spirit. We must now consider the human experience of spirit. I don't think it is possible to separate spirit from form. By the nature of our human evolution we have acquired transitional states of consciousness that allow us to enact the imaginary. We can enter altered states of consciousness through meditation, dream in reverie or fear, and think. The essence of spirit lies in the awakening of a higher conscious order that is best enabled when I meet you in relation.[469] This is what defines spirit. It is only when you and I create space and encounter each other meaningfully that we can engage spirit.[470] I think this is what Buber meant when he discussed our place in distance and relation.[471]

Spirit becomes the higher conscious order that emerges out of the synchronous activation of our salience network. It is the emergence of a higher order of function that can elicit in us the common experiences of empathy, compassion and love when we become unconditionally present for the other. The salience network through the anterior insula is involved in our ability to understand the emotional states of others by sharing their experience and their affective states.[472] More recently it has been shown that the salience network through the anterior insula and anterior cingulate cortex is active in states requiring complex social emotions involving compassion for physical and psychological pain.[473]

When we consciously become present for the other we strip ourselves to the *naked essentials of relation* and awaken the underpinnings of spirit. We beckon our inner spirit to emerge through our *intention* in the same way we turn to God in the Jewish tradition of kavanah.[474] It is *intention* to be present that activates salience and connects all the dots along the neural pathways of our brain that bring spirit to the "in-between." Spirit can emerge in the space we share because spirit is emergent in us. Out of the rooted vine of our inner self in the very structure of our brain there is spirit.

Spirit emerges because spirit is present. If we think of spirit in terms of the human structure of the brain the emergence of spirit becomes accessible. The human brain has ten to the tenth power neurons that fire and depolarize at quantum levels.[475] We do not have to stretch our imaginations too far to see that countless millions of neurons spontaneously firing and then entering the quantum state of ordered vibrational unity can emerge in what we may call spirit.[476,477] Vibrational unity is an ordered quantum state that supersedes our immediate physical senses. It is the world of spirit. It is the same world that creates the invisible matrix between us when we share our common space and we become unconditionally present for each other.

We can connect the dots between us because the dots are there in the spirit of relation.

I believe this is the world of the prophets and saints. It is the world of Isaiah, Ezekiel, Jeremiah, Daniel and Mohammed. It is the world from which Jesus was born and lives in the hearts and souls of many. We must recognize that our human capacity to experience spiritual states is grounded in the higher order of our brain's neurons. When I stand in relation to some other and I commit to become unconditionally present I enact a higher order of neural processing. I create the conditions that recruit the salience network and activate the deeper neural circuitry that enables spiritual experience. I call upon the spirit in me to meet the spirit in you across the chasm that separates us.

When we commit to unconditional presence for another we remove the veil from our ego and expose our inner self. It is this selfless vulnerability to be fully human with another that enacts the higher order of neural function that accesses spirit. If God is the spirit that lives within each of us then I believe it is our higher quantum order that allows God to be experienced. When we become less, God becomes more. We strip ourselves to the *naked essentials of relation* and this lowering of the veil activates a higher order which is the experience of God within us, *Emmanuel*.

It is the ordered quantum state that would explain our experience of the omniscience, omnipresence and omnipotence of God in us. It conveys how spirit can exist in the "in-between" and how we may be made worthy of the experience of spirit. In between our words, our thoughts, and in between you and I is spirit. It crosses the branches of the rooted vine and connects us out of the quantum state that emerges when I become less for you. Each time we create the intention to be unconditionally present we focus our faculties on the other who stands before us. This can transition our mental frame from our awake beta state to the more meditative alpha state.

This is what I mean by stripping ourselves to the *naked essentials of relation*. We humble ourselves in both body and spirit and we devote our whole being to the person who stands before us. We allow our demeanor to deflate in an effort toward humility and lower the chaotic rhythms of our mind. At that moment we stand on sacred ground. We stand on the soil of relation. This evolves to a reciprocal mindfulness of body, soul and spirit in a symbiotic bond of mutual relation.

When we exercise the *intention* to be present for the other we activate autonomously functioning neural networks that trigger specific responses in our brain. Our eyes will unconsciously capture visual streams of information that generate from the one who is before us and our eyes will respond in kind. Each movement of our eyes will coalesce into specific patterns of conjugate movements that will recruit ancillary neural circuits along the matrix of our mind. Our visual system has intricate neural connections to the *salience network* and through the amygdala it is directly tied to our limbic pathways.[478]

This is our implicit or archetypal language. It is the unconscious process by which I believe spirit emerges behind the veil of the ego. It is through our *intention* to be present that we abdicate all pretensions and allow spirit to emerge within and between us. We allow our deeper centers to direct us in relation to the other. Our brain is well equipped to guide us in our efforts to be present for the other. At the uppermost layer of our brain our cortex is arranged in both vertical and horizontal neural connections.[479] This cytoarchitecture creates multiple synaptic links to subpopulations of neurons in our brainstem, limbic system and most notably the salience network. Our cortical receptivity amplified by multiple cortical neuron clusters has the capacity to activate the salience network in response to our *intention*. Reciprocally, the hippocampus as part of the limbic system can generate a "reverberatory loop circuit"[480] to the neocortex completing the circuit. When I become present for the other it is through my *intention* to be present that I create the synaptic pathways necessary for unconditional presence. When I strip myself to the *naked essentials of relation* my body demeanor becomes physically humbled to the one before me. My reception by the other is a crucial determinant in closing the chasm between us that will further allow our continued dialogue in relation.

One must always remember that our demeanor is under constant scrutiny by the other's unconscious. The amygdala and its connection to cells within the superior temporal polysensory area are extremely sensitive to the sight and nuances of faces and facial expressions.[481] That is why our presence must be unconditional. It is only by the mindful attention to the other that we create the circumstances that engender receptivity by the other. We must also remember that our unconscious is also at work unconsciously processing what we may not be consciously perceiving. This is what I refer to as the *reciprocities of the unconscious*. This is what engenders the background pantomime of archetypal or implicit language. It becomes the unconscious dance along the invisible matrix between two people in serious dialogue. It is the spirit within and between that crosses the chasm and unites us in relation.

CHAPTER 19

RECIPROCITIES OF THE SPIRIT

I t is impossible to discuss the expression of spirit in human dialogue without considering the human matrix within which spirit is expressed. *Spirit and form*[482] embrace a fundamental relationship across the boundaries of our human consciousness. When I meet you in relation[483] and I am unconditionally present to you I enact a transcendent psychic function. It is a *transcendence*[484] that abates the control and confines of the ego and allows a higher order of relational receptivity to occur. This act of transcending the confines of the ego to be present for the other is an act of spirit.

The idea that this may be a psychologizing of the spirit has to be approached with broader parameters. When I am present for you it is because I have elicited the highest order of my neural development to beckon the spirit within me to become the spirit between I and you. Spirit becomes the gift of my higher human order. It is only within the matrix of psyche that spirit is present and manifest within us. When we hear terms such as the Holy Spirit, the Comforter, or Shekinah we don't need to separate *spirit and form*[485] and construct separate camps for each of them. The higher ideal is achieved when spirit and form become the unified body within us. This is the transcendence that allows spirit to emerge within and between us.

When we consider all the great religious and philosophical traditions we see one common thread that weaves through each of them. It is the thread of transcendence. Whether it is the Christian monk, Buddhist priest, or

Indian sage they each enact a meditative or prayerful practice to engage the spirit within. It is this spirit living in the psyche or soul of each of us that becomes the transcendent experience of relation. It is a reciprocity[486] of spirit when I am in relation with you. This is what separates the world of the mundane from the world of spirit. It is the difference between the I-It and the I-Thou.[487]

The reciprocity of spirit[488] is a relational dyad between the spirit in me and the spirit in you. It is an undercurrent of implicit or archetypal language that connects our souls and not just our minds. This reciprocity is possible only when the unconditional presence of relation[489] is embraced. It is the unconscious in me connecting the dots on the matrix between us, but it is the spirit within me that crosses along the branches of the rooted vine. This unconscious reciprocity is only possible through the act of devotion in relation. It is only through a selfless lowering of the veil of the ego that spirit emerges and offers the other the possibility of reciprocal dialogue.[490]

This is the great risk in all relation. Reciprocity always implies the risk that the space "in-between" will not be crossed or that the spirit will move along unrooted branches. All we can do is allow spirit to emerge and allow the presence of spirit to help heal the other's soul. This is the great task of relation. Buber has shown that a soul is never sick in isolation but always in relation to some other.[491] It is in the "betweenness,"[492] according to Buber, that the soul of one becomes sick in relation to the other. In my own work with patients I use three precepts that I always try to follow when I encounter another in dialogue. This, however, applies to anyone engaged in meaningful conversation. First and foremost is silence when I encounter another. This allows the other to contemplate their thoughts and allows the groundswell of spirit to emerge. My silence is their invitation to begin to process what needs to be said. I think of my silence as a retreat into the soul that engenders a meditative quietude. Buber wrote about silence in relation to the other as freeing the other "where the spirit does not manifest itself but is."[493]

If silence is to be silence in the spirit it must be accompanied with listening which is the second precept. It is important to listen to those who need to speak to us. When we listen to another we give them a chance to hear themselves speak which is often what they need in order to make sense of their thoughts. When they hear their own words spoken to someone who is truly mindful of them spirit emerges between the words.

It becomes the connecting link that bridges the chasm of ordinary space. Lastly, one must always be present[494] for the other if silence and listening is to be received in the spirit.

Spirit emerges when spirit is beckoned. It is our task to create the conditions that allow both the emergence and recognition of spirit to occur. Spirit is always present between and within us but lies in a solitary invisibility until it is beckoned. The condition from which spirit emerges is ultimately only through the hallowing of the soul that can sufficiently defuse the ego. When we humble ourselves in unconditional presence for the other we hallow the ground upon which we stand and make sacred the space between us. This engenders healing the inner soul and helps to free the mind of the problems it endures. It hallows and frees the other.

In this unfortunate time in our history we are perhaps unfamiliar with the idea of hallowing or making holy. Our preoccupations and chaos with the mundane have removed us from the sphere of the holy and have made concepts such as *unconditional presence* obsolete. Perhaps if we consider the cultural context of our lives and our need to drug and sedate our senses we will begin to better understand how far we have strayed from the holy. Corporate dogma has become the new golden calf that has torn the curtain and veil of our sacred space. We no longer enjoy the simple act of prayer or find consolation in *spirit*. We live and work under the stress of a corporate structure that has stifled our human creativity and has made our survival contingent upon the corporate model of the world. In too many ways our religions have violated our basic trust in them by transgressing the values and spiritual practices they profess. This, in my opinion, reflects what Jung termed enantiodromia[495] or the attraction of opposites.

Jung made the point that whenever our conscious mind strays too far from the balance of power in our unconscious mind there is an emergence of implicit unconscious energy.[496] The emergence of the unconscious in this context is often associated with catastrophic consequences. When there is a general feeling that something has gone awry and we can no longer understand or make sense of our behaviors and actions this is a telltale sign of the emergence of the unconscious. This activity can be personal or collective. It may occur when an individual is simply out of sorts, but it can also happen when a country or world is out of sorts. The consequences in this regard are usually far more serious.

Someone recently asked me if I thought anything could be done to correct the great imbalance in our world politics. She was distraught about the clamor over our challenges with immigration, terrorism, homelessness, and poverty. She felt overwhelmed by not being able to do more but she conscientiously did everything she could to help those she encountered. As we talked in the quiet of my treatment room there emerged an unspoken aura that surrounded us. It felt as if *spirit* had emerged. We suddenly knew that it was only *spirit* that could resolve the problems we discussed. Each person had to do exactly what *she* was doing every day that she awoke. She became *unconditionally present* for the homeless man on the street in the same way that she was unconditionally present for me.

Spirit emerges in the space we share when we begin to balance the great divide within us. When we discover imbalances in the world we need to look within ourselves for the imbalances within us. Until we recognize that our divide is the world's divide we are paralyzed in our capacity to help anyone. Spirit emerges both within and between us when the great divide between our conscious and unconscious mind enacts the path of reconciliation. This is the great balance. Spirit emerges in the space we share with another and closes the chasm between us but only when spirit can emerge in the space within us and close the chasm of our mind.

Spirit needs us to do the work of personal reconciliation so that we can mend the inner wounds that we all endure. When we reconcile our inner world we reconcile the space we share.

CHAPTER 20

CROSSING THE GREAT DIVIDE

In the previous chapter I spoke about the transcendent function as introduced by Jung in his work in analytical psychology. Transcendence as an experience of everyday life, however, is often considered by many to be an unachievable practice. So how are we to pursue this practice if it is imperative to the unconditional presence of relation?[497] Abraham Joshua Heschel believed that the greatest work of the human being was to emulate God's self-transcendence so that we transcend ourselves.[498] I realize that such aspirations may be considered extraordinary, but this is where I believe we have displaced our values to the more egocentric views of the world.

Each person is an absolute microcosm of the greater world and through a single act of transcendence we all can be transformative. It is impossible to conjure acts of transcendence and transformation without conjuring the presence of God in the spirit of relation.[499] Transcendence and transformation exist in a reciprocal relationship predicated upon a *healing space*.[500] It is only by overcoming our ego's consuming drive for self-indulgence that we can create an *empty space*[501] that allows the presence of spirit or God to emerge.[502]

This empty space is an opening of the inner psychic space[503] that presides within the vast domain of our deeper unconscious. It is the space that the unconscious has evolved from its earliest beginnings in the in-utero baby where silence[504] is syntonic with spirit. Recently, I had an experience where silence and the emergence of spirit became overwhelmingly self-evident. I was in the treatment room with Rob, a middle-aged man whom I had known for many years. He recently lost his close friend in a traffic accident and his death affected him in ways he hadn't expected. During our ordinary conversation I noticed his eyes swelling with tears and I became silent.

My silence seemed to open the space between us that somehow separated us from the greater world. It was spirit in the *in-between*[505] unequivocally present. I listened in silence and I realized that a transcendence and transformation was evolving in the healing space we shared. I could sense an actual presence that embodied our relation and I knew that the healing spirit crossed the branches of the rooted vine between us.

As Rob left the office that day he placed his hand upon my shoulder and quietly embraced me. "Thank you," he said, "I feel so much better." It was in the silence of our encounter that our implicit unspoken language[506] became the language of spirit. This is how we cross the great divide that separates us. We soften the spoken word, peel away the veil of the ego and allow spirit to emerge.

It is only by emptying ourselves that we open our inner space where spirit lives and God can "be."[507] What we unfortunately fail to realize is how our present culture has indoctrinated us in ego driven ideals. Each instance of preoccupation with our overly material acquisitions separates us and widens the divide between us. Spirit has been clandestinely abducted from our inner space and replaced with the clutter of contemporary life. Until we can transcend the ego ideals we have been lured to love we will have great difficulty creating space for spirit to live and cross the great divide. The message I get when reading Heschel is that *prayer is the way we transcend the self and by focusing on God we express God.*[508]

This is the spirit in relation.[509] The less self-absorbed we become the more we can recognize spirit. Buber wrote that spirit exists "not in the I but between I and You"[510] and he compared it to "like the air in which you breathe."[511] Although I firmly believe that spirit lives in the *between* I also see spirit existing in each of us and within the invisible matrix between us. Spirit is there and connects us as we connect the dots between us. If spirit is like the air we breathe then spirit is as much a part of our inner sanctum as we are a part of spirit. Healing occurs within and between us when we are unconditionally accepted in our totality for who we are.[512] This idea may go further than we realize. In paraphrasing Buber, it requires us to fully receive the other without denuding them of their most basic functions and flaws.[513] It is this conditionality that is the essence of our alienation. This, I believe, is partly what Buber meant when he stated that we never get sick alone "but always through a betweenness" with our self and some other.[514]

The work of medicine and psychotherapy must be reexamined from the perspective of the I-Thou relationship.[515] All too often the sick and suffering are received in an atmosphere of overwhelming conditionality. Our institutionalized model of care has largely replaced our capacity for the *unconditional presence* that is often required for inner healing. Until we examine ourselves in totality and understand our own capacity to be fully present for another we will be unable to make positive change. *Unconditional presence* is a process. It requires an inner orientation not to the world but to the world of others. It is an inner disposition or state of being that is enacted in relation when we strip away the veil of the ego and allow spirit to emerge.

In a sense we must become self-transcendent.[516] We must return to the *naked essentials of relation* where our bare essentiality is the only thing offered in relation. We strip the frivolities of the ego and we find the beauty[517] of spirit. This is the essence of unconditional relation. It is the emergence and movement of spirit across the chasm between us. It is what links us in our basic essentiality. What we fail to see is what is obvious before our eyes. We are so far removed from our inner spirit that we have no consciousness of its place in our lives. We have crushed our spirit under the weight of our acquisitions and fail to see spirit in the one who stands before us.

There is the great divide that separates us. It is a cluttered domain that fills the space we share and prevents the spirit in me from crossing the chasm to the spirit in you. In Shai Held's book on Abraham Joshua Heschel, *The call of transcendence*, he discusses Heschel's views on prayer being a way to "open a door" for God and the soul to enter.[518] In my view this is the essence of spirit and how spirit crosses the chasm between us. Prayer sweeps away the invisible clutter that separates us and fills the space "between I and You."[519] There is no way to extricate spirit from the domain of the *between* because it is in the *between* that the mystery of spirit presides.[520]

Each time we encounter each other unconditionally we participate in unraveling this mystery.[521] This is how we connect spirit across the rooted vine. I allow myself to become enamoured by the mysterious[522] in the same way a young child is enamoured gazing at the stars on a moonlit night. It is only with total wonder[523] that the experience of God in Spirit can be made visible across the chasms between us. Perhaps we have to become as little children[524] to accomplish this sense of wonder and cross the great divide. Each time we encounter another it is only through the lens of the mysterious[525] that we can experience the wonder[526] of our space and the emergence of our spirit. To my way of thinking, it is Heschel's sense of wonder[527] that makes a significant contribution to the *betweenness*[528] of our personal encounters. It is our loss of *wonder* that blunts our inclination to experience the space in-between "I and You."[529]

Perhaps it is time to embrace the *mysterious*. It is only through the mystery of *"I and You"* that the mystery of spirit emerges.[530] We must begin to see beyond the clutter of our world and see the majesty of the between. The space we share is the body of spirit and by engaging each other unconditionally we share in spirit.[531]

CHAPTER 21

A THEOLOGY OF SPIRIT

I hope this book in some small way casts a light on the wonder[532] and mystery[533] that exists between us when we meet. In my own work I have enjoyed the mystery of spirit between my patients and I in ways that I could never have imagined. It was these experiences that became the driving force in my quest to answer many of the questions I have raised in this book. Early in my academic career I knew there was much more to a healing encounter than ordering the right test or prescribing the right treatment. Each encounter was special. It was an experience in relation.[534]

In the earliest days of my undergraduate studies I discovered the works of Martin Buber and Carl Jung but must admit that my initial introduction to their work was overwhelming. The philosophy of Buber intrigued me but the depth of his philosophical ideas was daunting. What Buber presented on a philosophical and theological level Jung just as dauntingly presented on a psychological level, but for some reason I couldn't let their work go. I began repetitively reading Buber's "I and Thou" trying to grasp the deeper implications of his ideas and at the same time began an in depth study of Jungian psychology.

As I evolved in my career and work with patients I began to see that there was a "theology of spirit" that existed in every encounter. Buber has more than adequately defined this in his many works on psychology and psychotherapy,[535] but I don't know if the word "theology" was ever actually used in this context. I know of no better way, however, to define the emergence of spirit in relation[536] as defined by Buber than the idea of an actual theology of spirit. It was the idea of this underlying theology in patient encounters that seemed to bring greater depth to the healing of each patient.

Each encounter was more than psychology and more than philosophy but what was it? There was always something in the underbelly of every serious encounter that engendered a higher order. The more deeply I invested myself in trying to understand the suffering of another the more I came to realize that there was something "between"[537] and within us that was at work. It was spirit in the "between"[538] as Buber defined it but it was also spirit across the domain of psyche as Jung discovered it in his transcendent function.[539]

Spirit and form[540] can not be separated from a human being. It is form[541] in the properties of our higher neural integration that allows the expression of spirit across the expanse of our mind. On many occasions Heschel raised the point that God is in search of man because God is a partner in the terrestrial world of man and needs him to fulfill the work of His creation.[542] Perhaps we have removed ourselves from the investment God made in us. By overly focusing on the world of "It" we delude ourselves into a false sense of security and constrict the distance between us.[543,544] We allow distance to "enlarge and thicken"[545] so that the "in-between" is no longer sacred space but ordinary space and the world of "It."[546]

Life in the present day has evolved into an extensive alphabet of ideologies and pseudo-beliefs. They constrict our distance[547] and muddle the space we share by removing us from meaningful dialogue. This then hampers our ability to detach from these intangible doctrines which become another gadget that invisibly clutters our mind and exiles our spirit. Our world has slowly and deceptively displaced God from our inner space.

A theology of spirit is a theology of "I and You."[548] To my way of thinking, each encounter that we have is an encounter with the world. When I meet you in relation[549] I encounter you fully[550] and allow our shared space to evolve. The difference between encountering you fully and encountering you conditionally is that I receive you without preconceived notions or preconceptions. My ideologies are eliminated from our orbit of relation and I receive you as you are.[551] Once I begin to psychologize you or try to understand the motivations for our encounter I have fled into the world of "It"[552] and the orbit of our relation is eliminated. I have sacrified the theology of spirit on the alter of conditionality.

Jung, in his reply to Buber in relation to the God-image, stood firmly on his belief that the God-image was an "autonomous psychic content" that can "burst upon the ego" as a "living experience."[553] This is the divine spark in each of us. It is our theology of spirit in the flesh that allows the sprit of relation to exist.

ENDNOTES

1. Friedman, M. Martin Buber: The life of dialogue. 4th ed. London and New York. Routledge. 2002, 98–113.
2. Ibid., 98–113.
3. Praglin, L. (2006). The Nature of the "In-Between" in D.W. Winnicott's Concept of Transitional Space and in Martin Buber's das Zwischenmenschliche. Universitas, Vol. 2 Issue 2 (Fall 2006) accessed on-line at www.uni.edu/universitas/archive/fall 06/pdf/art_praglin.pdf.
4. Perri, Vincent. The healing space. Understanding the true nature of inner healing. Boca Raton. Universal-Publishers. 2014, 51–55.
5. Buber, Martin. I-thou. (W. Kaufmann, Trans.). New York. Charles Scribner's sons: 1970, 126–137.
6. Perri, Vincent. Conjugate gaze adjustive technique: An introduction to innovative chiropractic theory and practice. USA. Universal Publishers. 2001, 93–94.
7. Praglin, L. (2006). The Nature of the "In-Between" in D.W. Winnicott's Concept of Transitional Space and in Martin Buber's das Zwischenmenschliche. Universitas, Vol. 2 Issue 2 (Fall 2006) accessed on-line at www.uni.edu/universitas/archive/fall 06/pdf/art_praglin.pdf.
8. Perri, Vincent. Conjugate gaze adjustive technique: An introduction to innovative chiropractic theory and practice. USA. Universal Publishers. 2001, 93–94.

9. Perri, Vincent. Conjugate gaze adjustive technique: An introduction to innovative chiropractic theory and practice. USA. Universal Publishers. 2001, 93–94.

10. Perri, Vincent. Language of the archetype. Explorations of the unconscious in movement, speech, and development. Bethel, Ct. Rutledge Books, Inc.: 1997, 119.

11. Buber, Martin. I-thou. (W. Kaufmann, Trans.). New York. Charles Scribner's sons: 1970, 116.

12. Jung, C.G. Psychology and alchemy. 2nd ed. (R.F.C. Hull, Trans.). Princeton. Princeton University Press. Bollingen Series xx. 1953, 182–183.

13. Ibid., 182–183.

14. Buber, M. I and thou. (W. Kaufmann, Trans.). New York. Charles Scribner's sons: 1970, 116.

15. Friedman, M. Martin Buber: The life of dialogue. 4th ed. London and New York. Routledge. 2002, 98–113.

16. Perri, Vincent. The healing space. Understanding the true nature of inner healing. Boca Raton. Universal-Publishers. 2014, 29–35.

17. Ibid., 51–55.

18. Buber, Martin. I and thou. (W. Kaufmann, Trans.). New York. Charles Scribner's sons: 1970, 116.

19. Ibid., 1970, 116.

20. Chamberlain, David. The fetal senses: A classical view. Birth psychology. Accessed on-line 07/12/2013 at http://birthpsychology.com/free-article/fetal-senses-classical-view.

21. Ibid.

22. Chamberlain, David. The fetal senses: A classical view. Birth psychology. Accessed on-line 07/12/2013 at http://birthpsychology.com/free-article/fetal-senses-classical-view.

23. Perri, Vincent. The healing space. Understanding the true nature of inner healing. Boca Raton. Universal-Publishers. 2014, 29–35.

24. Buber, Martin. I and thou. (W. Kaufmann, Trans.). New York. Chares Scribner's sons: 1970, 116.

25. Perri, Vincent. The healing space. Understanding the true nature of inner healing. Boca Raton. Universal-Publishers. 2014, 29–35.

26. Ibid., 29–35.

27. Buber, Martin. I and Thou. (Walter Kaufmann, trans.). New York. Charles Scribner's sons. 1970, 89.

28. Ibid., 116.

29. Buber, Martin. I and thou. (W. Kaufmann, Trans.). New York. Charles Scribner's sons: 1970, 62.

30. Ibid., 53–57.

31. Buber, Martin. I and thou. (W. Kaufmann, Trans.). New York. Charles Scribner's sons. 1970, 62.

32. Ibid., 116.

33. Buber, Martin. I and thou. (W. Kaufmann, Trans.). New York. Charles Scribner's sons. 1970, 62.

34. Ibid., 53–57.

35. Samuels, Andrew. Jung and the post-Jungians. London and New York: Tavistock/Routledge: 1985, 58–60.

36. Perri, Vincent. The healing space. Understanding the true nature of inner healing. Boca Raton. Universal-Publishers. 2014, 29–35.

37. Samuels, Andrew. Jung and the post-Jungians. London and New York. Tavistock/Routledge: 1985, 58–60.

38. Ibid., 58–60.

39. Samuels, Andrew. Jung and the post-Jungians. London and New York. Tavistock/Routledge: 1985, 58–60.

40. Buber, Martin. I and thou. (W. Kaufmann, Trans.). New York. Charles Scribner's sons. 1970, 116.

41. Ibid., 53–57.

42. Buber, Martin. I and thou. (W. Kaufmann, Trans.). New York. Charles Scribner's sons. 1970, 136–143.

43. Ibid., 130.

44. Buber, Martin. I and thou. (W. Kaufmann, Trans.). New York. Charles Scribner's sons. 1970, 130.

45. Perri, Vincent. Conjugate gaze somato-emotional release. A novel approach to physiotherapeutic mind-body therapy. USA. Universal Publishers. 2014, 81.

46. Friedman, M. Martin Buber: The life of dialogue. 4th ed. London and New York. Routledge. 2002, 98–113.

47. Perri, Vincent. The healing space. Understanding the true nature of inner healing. Boca Raton. Universal-Publishers. 2014, 51–55.

48. Matthew 26:36–46.

49. Praglin, L. (2006). The Nature of the "In-Between" in D.W. Winnicott's Concept of Transitional Space and in Martin Buber's das Zwischenmenschliche. Universitas, Vol. 2 Issue 2 (Fall 2006) accessed on-line at www.uni.edu/universitas/archive/fall 06/pdf/art_praglin.pdf.

50. Matthew 26:36–46.
51. Buber, Martin. I and thou. (W. Kaufmann, Trans.). New York. Charles Scribner's sons. 1970, 116.
52. Ibid., 116.
53. Buber, Martin. On Judaism. Ed. Nahum N. Glatzer. New York. Schocken Books. 1967, 4.
54. Ibid., 4.
55. Jung, C.G. Psychology and alchemy. 2nd ed. (R.F.C. Hull, Trans.). Princeton. Princeton University Press. Bollingen series xx. 1953, 182–183.
56. Buber, Martin. I and thou. (Walter Kaufmann, Trans.). New York. Charles Scribner's sons. 1970, 53–57.
57. Perri, Vincent. The healing space. Understanding the true nature of inner healing. Boca Raton. Universal-Publishers. 2014, 64.
58. Buber, Martin. I and thou. (Walter Kaufmann, Trans.). New York. Charles Scribner's and sons. 1970, 63–64, 107.
59. Ibid., 63–64, 107.
60. Buber, Martin. I and Thou. (Walter Kaufmann, trans.). New York. Charles Scribner's sons. 1970, 89.
61. Ibid., 127.
62. Matthew 26:36–46.
63. Buber, Martin. On Judaism. Ed. Nahum N. Glatzer. New York. Schocken Books. 1967, 70.
64. Matthew 26:36–46.
65. Friedman, M. Martin Buber: The life of dialogue. 4th ed. London and New York. Routledge. 2002, 84–97.
66. Andrews, Samuels. Jung and the post-Jungians. London and New York. Tavistock/Routledge: 1985, 58–60.
67. Buber, Martin. I and thou. (Walter Kaufmann, Trans.). New York. Charles Scribner's sons. 1970, 63–64, 107.
68. Friedman, M. Martin Buber: The life of dialogue. 4th ed. London and New York. Routledge. 2002, 84–97.
69. Buber, Martin. I and thou. (Walter Kaufmann, Trans.). New York. Charles Scribner's sons. 1970, 116.
70. Ibid., 54–85.
71. Ibid., 89.
72. Buber, Martin. I and thou. (Walter Kaufmann, Trans.). New York. Charles Scribner's sons. 1970, 89.
73. Perri, V. Conjugate gaze somato-emotional release. A novel approach to physiotherapeutic mind-body therapy. Universal Publishers. USA. 2014, 81.

74. Ibid., 81.

75. Buber, Martin. I and thou. (Walter Kaufmann, Trans.). New York. Charles Scribner's sons. 1970, 63–64, 107.

76. Perri, Vincent. The healing space: Understanding the true nature of inner healing. Boca Raton. Universal-Publishers. 2014.

77. Praglin, L. (2006). The Nature of the "In-Between" in D.W. Winnicott's Concept of Transitional Space and in Martin Buber's das Zwischenmenschliche. Universitas, Vol. 2 Issue 2 (Fall 2006) accessed on-line at www.uni.edu/ universitas/archive/fall 06/pdf/art_praglin.pdf.

78. Buber, Martin. I and thou. (Walter Kaufmann, Trans.). New York. Charles Scribner's sons. 1970, 63–64, 107.

79. Ibid., 63–64, 107.

80. Friedman, M. Martin Buber: The life of dialogue. 4th ed. London and New York. Routledge. 2002, 98–113.

81. Ibid., 201.

82. Buber, Martin. I and thou. (Walter Kaufmann, Trans.). New York. Charles Scribner's sons. 1970, 63–64, 107.

83. Friedman, M. Martin Buber: The life of dialogue. 4th ed. London and New York. Routledge. 2002, 98–113.

84. Buber, Martin. I and thou. (Walter Kaufmann, Trans.). New York. Charles Scribner's sons. 1970, 53–85.

85. Ibid., 107.

86. John 14:26.

87. John 14:16.

88. Buber, Martin. I and thou. (Walter Kaufmann, Trans.). New York. Charles Scribner's sons. 1970, 53–85.

89. Friedman, M. Martin Buber: The life of dialogue. 4th ed. London and New York. Routledge. 2002, 85.

90. Buber, Martin. I and thou. (Walter Kaufmann, Trans.). New York. Charles Scribner's sons. 1970, 116.

91. Friedman, M. Martin Buber: The life of dialogue. 4th ed. London and New York. Routledge. 2002, 85.

92. Job 32:8.

93. Buber, Martin. On Judaism. Ed. Nahum N. Glatzer. New York. Schocken Books. 1967, 28.

94. Ibid., 28.

95. Samuels, Andrew. Jung and the post-Jungians. London and New York. Tavistock/Routledge. 1985, 92–94.

96. Ibid., 58–60.

97. Samuels, Andrew. Jung and the post-Jungians. London and New York. Tavistock/Routledge. 1985, 58–60.

98. Buber, Martin. On Judaism. Ed. Nahum N. Glatzer. New York. Schocken Books. 1967, 28.

99. Buber, Martin. I and thou. (Walter Kaufmann, Trans.). New York. Charles Scribner's sons. 1970, 89.

100. Ibid., 116.

101. Agassi, Judith Buber, ed. Martin Buber on psychology and psychotherapy: Essays, lectures, and dialogue. USA. Syracuse University Press. 1999, 201–224.

102. Buber, Martin. On Judaism. Ed. Nahum N. Glatzer. New York. Schocken Books. 1967, 28.

103. Perri, Vincent. The healing space: Understanding the true nature of inner healing. Boca Raton. Universal-Publishers. 2014, 63–66.

104. Buber, Martin. I and thou. (Walter Kaufmann, Trans.). New York. Charles Scribner's sons. 1970, 116.

105. Ibid., 89.

106. Buber, Martin. I and thou. (Walter Kaufmann, Trans.). New York. Charles Scribner's sons. 1970, 89.

107. Ibid., 89.

108. Buber, Martin. I and thou. (Walter Kaufmann, Trans.). New York. Charles Scribner's sons. 1970, 116.

109. Buber, Martin. On Judaism. Ed. Nahum N. Glatzer. New York. Schocken Books. 1967, 29–30.

110. Buber, Martin. I and thou. (Walter Kaufmann, Trans.). New York. Charles Scribner's sons. 1970, 89.

111. Ibid., 62.

112. Matthew 5:4.

113. Buber, Martin. I and thou. (Walter Kaufmann, Trans.). New York. Charles Scribner's sons. 1970, 62.

114. Buber, Martin. On Judaism. Ed. Nahum. N. Glatzer. New York. Schocken Books. 1967, 29–30.

115. Buber, Martin. I and thou. (Walter Kaufmann, Trans.). New York. Charles Scribner's sons. 1970, 62.

116. Ibid., 116.

117. Jung, Carl. The essential Jung: Selected writings introduced by Anthony Storr. Princeton, New Jersey. Princeton University Press. 1983, 13–14.

118. Buber, Martin. On Judaism. Ed. Nahum N. Glatzer. New York. Schocken Books. 1967, 29–30.

119. Buber, Martin. I and thou. (Walter Kaufmann, Trans.). New York. Charles Scribner's sons. 1970, 62.

120. Ibid., 116.

121. Buber, Martin. I and Thou. (Walter Kaufmann, trans.). New York. Charles Scribner's sons. 1970, 89.

122. Ibid., 63–64, 107.

123. Buber, Martin. I and thou. (Walter Kaufmann, Trans.). New York. Charles Scribner's sons. 1970, 63–64, 107.

124. Ibid., 53–85.

125. Buber, Martin. I and thou. (Walter Kaufmann, Trans.). New York. Charles Scribner's sons. 1970, 116.

126. Perri, Vincent. Language of the archetype: Explorations of the unconscious in movement, speech and development. Bethel, Ct. Rutledge Books, Inc.: 1997.

127. Buber, Martin. I and thou. (Walter Kaufmann, Trans.). New York. Charles Scribner's sons. 1970, 116.

128. Ibid., 63–64, 107.

129. Perri, Vincent. Language of the archetype: Explorations of the unconscious in movement, speech and development. Bethel, Ct. Rutledge Books, Inc.: 1997, 128–129.

130. Friedman, Maurice S. Martin Buber: The Life of Dialogue. 4th ed. London and New York. Routledge. 1955, 98–113.

131. Perri, Vincent. Language of the archetype: Explorations of the unconscious in movement, speech and development. Bethel, Ct. Rutledge Books, Inc.: 1997, 128–129.

132. Buber, Martin. I and thou. (Walter Kaufmann, Trans.). New York. Charles Scribner's sons. 1970, 116.

133. Ibid., 53–85.

134. Perri, Vincent. Language of the archetype: Explorations of the unconscious in movement, speech and development. Bethel, Ct. Rutledge Books, Inc.: 1997, 128–129.

135. Buber, Martin. I and thou. (Walter Kaufmann, Trans.). New York. Charles Scribner's sons. 1970, 116.

136. Ibid., 116.

137. Buber, Martin. I and thou. (Walter Kaufmann, Trans.). New York. Charles Scribner's sons. 1970, 107.

138. Perri, V. Language of the archetype: Explorations of the unconscious in movement, speech and development. Bethel, Ct. Rutledge Books, Inc.: 1997.

139. Steckley, L. (2005). Therapeutic containment and holding environments: Understanding and reducing physical restraint in residential child care. Accessed on-line at www.celcis.org/media/resources/publications/PR_and_Containment.

140. Perri, Vincent. Conjugate gaze somato-emotional release. A novel approach to physiotherapeutic mind-body therapy. Universal Publishers. USA. 2014, 81.

141. Steckley, L. (2005). Therapeutic containment and holding environment: Understanding and reducing physical restraint in residential child care. Accessed on-line at www.celcis.org/media/resources/publications/PR_and_Containment.

142. Buber, Martin. I and thou. (Walter Kaufmann, Trans.). New York. Charles Scribner's sons. 1970, 116.

143. Ibid., 137.

144. Friedman, M. Martin Buber: The life of dialogue. 4th ed. London and New York. Routledge. 1955, 98–113.

145. Steckley, L. (2005). Therapeutic containment and holding environment: Understanding and reducing physical restraint in residential child care. Accessed on-line at www.celcis.org/media/resources/publications/PR_and_Containment.

146. Buber, Martin. I and thou. (Walter Kaufmann, Trans.). New York. Charles Scribner's sons. 1970, 107.

147. Ibid., 107.

148. Buber, Martin. I and thou. (Walter Kaufmann, Trans.). New York. Charles Scribner's sons. 1970, 107.

149. Ibid., 107.

150. Winnicott, D.W. (1986). Holding and interpretation. London. Hogarth Press. Referenced on-line at http://modernpsychoanalysis.org/. James G. Fennessy, M.A., J.D. Matawan, N.J. 07747. Copyright. 2007.

151. Buber, Martin. I and thou. (Walter Kaufmann, Trans.). New York. Charles Scribner's sons. 1970, 107.

152. Samuels, Andrew. Jung and the post Jungians. London and New York. Tavistock/Routledge: 1985, 200.

153. Buber, Martin. I and thou. (Walter Kaufmann, Trans.). New York. Charles Scribner's sons. 1970, 62.

154. Friedman, M. Martin Buber: The life of dialogue. 4th ed. London and New York. Routledge. 1955, 98–113.

155. Buber, M. I and thou. (Walter Kaufmann, Trans.). New York. Charles Scribner's sons. 1970, 62.

156. Friedman, M. Martin Buber: The life of dialogue. 4th ed. London and New York. Routledge. 1955, 74.

157. Ibid., 74.

158. Friedman, M. Martin Buber: The life of dialogue. 4th ed. London and New York. Routledge. 1955, 98–113.

159. Buber, M. I and thou. (Walter Kaufmann, Trans.). New York. Charles Scribner's sons. 1970, 107.

160. Ibid., 62.

161. Buber, M. I and thou. (Walter Kaufmann, Trans.). New York. Charles Scribner's sons. 1970, 107.

162. Ibid., 89.

163. Buber, M. I and thou. (Walter Kaufmann, Trans.). New York. Charles Scribner's sons. 1970, 116.

164. Ibid., 89.

165. Perri, Vincent. The healing space: Understanding the true nature of inner healing. Boca Raton. Universal-Publishers. 2014, 63–66.

166. Buber, M. I and thou. (Walter Kaufmann, Trans.). New York. Charles Scribner's sons. 1970, 89.

167. Ibid., 89.

168. Buber, M. I and thou. (Walter Kaufmann, Trans.). New York. Charles Scribner's sons. 1970, 62.

169. Friedman, M. Martin Buber: The life of dialogue. 4th ed. London and New York. Routledge. 1955, 98–113.

170. Perri, Vincent. The healing space: Understanding the true nature of inner healing. Boca Raton. Universal-Publishers. 2014, 63–66.

171. Ibid., 31.

172. Buber, Martin. I and thou. (Walter Kaufmann, Trans.). New York. Charles Scribner's sons. 1970, 116.

173. Ibid., 89.

174. Buber, Martin. I and thou. (Walter Kaufmann, Trans.). New York. Charles Scribner's sons. 1970, 127.

175. Friedman, M. Martin Buber: The life of dialogue. 4th ed. London and New York. Routledge. 1955, 199–200.

176. Buber, Martin. I and thou. (Walter Kaufmann, Trans.). New York. Charles Scribner's sons. 1970, 137.

177. Ibid., 137.

178. Buber, Martin. I and thou. (Walter Kaufmann, Trans.). New York. Charles Scribner's sons. 1970, 116.

179. John 15:5.
180. Buber, Martin. On Judaism. Ed. Nahum N. Glatzer. New York. Schocken Books. 1967, 28.
181. Ibid., 85–86.
182. Buber, Martin. On Judaism. Ed. Nahum N. Glatzer. New York. Schocken Books. 1967, 85–86.
183. Friedman, M. Martin Buber: The life of dialogue. 4th ed. London and New York. Routledge. 1955, 201.
184. Buber, Martin. On Judaism. Ed. Nahum N. Glatzer. New York. Schocken Books. 1967, 85–86.
185. Buber, Martin. I and thou. (Walter Kaufmann, Trans.). New York. Charles Scribner's sons. 1970, 53–85.
186. Ibid., 116.
187. Buber, Martin. I and thou. (Walter Kaufmann, Trans.). New York. Charles Scribner's sons. 1979, 89.
188. Ibid., 62.
189. Jung, C.G. Psychology and alchemy. 2nd ed. (R.F.C. Hull, Trans.). Princeton. Princeton University Press. Bollingen series. Xx. 1953, 23.
190. Buber, Martin. I and thou. (Walter Kaufmann, Trans.). New York. Charles Scribner's sons. 1970, 89.
191. Friedman, M. Martin Buber: The life of dialogue. 4th ed. London and New York. Routledge. 1955, 200–201.
192. Ibid., 200.
193. Samuels, Andrew. Jung and the post Jungians. London and New York: Tavistock/Routledge: 1985, 212.
194. Buber, Martin. I and thou. (Walter Kaufmann, Trans.). New York. Charles Scribner's sons. 1970, 116.
195. Ibid., 116.
196. Friedman, M. Martin Buber. The life of dialogue. 4th ed. London and New York. Routledge. 1955, 200–201.
197. Samuels, Andrew. Jung and the post Jungians. London and New York: Tavistock/Rutledge: 1985, 212.
198. Friedman, M. Martin Buber. The life of dialogue. 4th ed. London and New York. Rutledge. 1955, 200–201.
199. Matthew 11:29.
200. Ibid., 200–201.
201. Buber, Martin. I and thou. (Walter Kaufmann, Trans.). New York. Charles Scribner's sons. 1970, 116.
202. Ibid., 127.

203. Buber, Martin. I and thou. (Walter Kaufmann, Trans.). New York. Charles Scribner's sons. 1970, 89.

204. Buber, M. Martin Buber on Psychology and Psychotherapy: Essays, letters, and dialogue. Ed. Judith Buber Agassi. Syracuse University Press. 1999, 21.

205. Friedman, M. Martin Buber: The life of dialogue. 4th ed. London and New York. Routledge. 1955, 155–173.

206. Ibid., 158–159.

207. Friedman, M. Martin Buber: The life of dialogue. 4th ed. London and New York. Routledge. 1955, 119.

208. Ibid., 119.

209. Friedman, M. Martin Buber. The life of dialogue. 4th ed. London and New York. Routledge. 1955, 22, 156.

210. Ibid., 162–163.

211. Perri, V. Conjugate gaze adjustive technique. An introduction to innovative chiropractic theory and practice. Universal Publishers. USA. 2001, 95.

212. Matthew 18:20.

213. The Zohar: Pritzker Edition, Volume One. Matt, Daniel C. Stanford. Stanford University Press. 2004, LXXIII.

214. Friedman, M. Martin Buber. The life of dialogue. 4th ed. London and New York. Routledge. 1955, 200–201.

215. Perri, V. Conjugate gaze adjustive technique. An introduction to innovative chiropractic theory and practice. Universal Publishers. USA. 2001, 95.

216. Buber, M. I and thou. (W. Kaufmann, Trans.). New York. Charles Scribner's sons. 1970, 89.

217. Perri, V. Language of the archetype. Explorations of the unconscious in movement, speech and development. Bethel, Connecticut. Rutledge Books, Inc. 1997, 122–123.

218. Buber, M. I and thou. (W. Kaufmann, Trans.). New York. Charles Scribner's sons. 1970, 116.

219. Jung, C.G. Psychology and alchemy. 2nd ed. (R.F.C. Hull, Tans.). Princeton. Princeton University Press. Bollingen series xx. 1953, 230–231.

220. Buber, M. I and thou. (W. Kaufmann, Trans.). New York. Charles Scribner's sons. 1970, 137.

221. Jung, C.G. Psychology and alchemy. 2nd ed. (R.F.C. Hull, Trans.). Princeton. Princeton University Press. Bollingen series xx. 1953, 159.

222. Samuels, A. Jung and the post-Jungians. London and New York: Tavistock/ Routledge: 1985, 212.

223. Ibid., 32.

224. Samuels, A. Jung and the post-Jungians. London and New York: Tavistock/ Routledge: 1985, 233.

225. Buber, M. I and thou. (W. Kaufmann, Trans.). New York. Charles Scribner's sons. 1970, 128.

226. Samuels, A. Jung and the post-Jungians. London and New York: Tavistock/ Routledge: 1985, 25.

227. Ibid., 29.

228. Jung, C. G. Psychology and alchemy. 2nd ed. (R.F.C. Hull, Trans.). Princeton. Princeton University Press. Bollingen series xx. 1953, 42.

229. Ibid., 166.

230. Samuels, A. Jung and the post-Jungians. London and New York: Tavistock/ Routledge: 1985, 32.

231. Ibid., 44–46.

232. Buber, M. On Judaism. Ed. Nahum N. Glatzer. New York. Schocken Books. 1967, 84–85.

233. Friedman, M. Martin Buber. The life of dialogue. 4th ed. London and New York. Routledge. 1955, 200–201.

234. Buber, M. I and thou. (Walter Kaufmann, Trans.). New York. Charles Scribner's sons. 1970, 89.

235. Ibid., 141.

236. The Zohar: Pritzker Edition, Volume one. Matt, Daniel C. Stanford. Stanford University Press. 2003, LIII.

237. Buber, M. On Judaism. Ed. Nahum N. Glatzer. New York. Schocken Books. 1967, 43.

238. Ibid., 43.

239. Buber, M. I and thou. (Walter Kaufmann, Trans.). New York. Charles Scribner's sons. 1970, 89.

240. Buber, M. On Judaism. Ed. Nahum N. Glatzer. New York. Schocken Books. 1967, 85.

241. Ibid., 85–86.

242. Jung, C. G. Psychology and alchemy. 2nd ed. (R. F. C. Hull, Trans.). Princeton. Princeton University Press. Bollingen series xx. 1953, 42.

243. Buber, M. I and thou. (Walter Kaufmann, Trans.). New York. Charles Scribner's sons. 1970, 67.

244. Ibid., 89.

245. Buber, M. I and thou. (Walter Kaufmann, Trans.). New York. Charles Scribner's sons. 1970, 137.

246. Ibid., 137.

247. Buber, M. I and thou. (Walter Kaufmann, Trans.). New York. Charles Scribner's sons. 1970, 107, 116.

248. Ibid., 67.

249. Perri, V. Language of the archetype. Explorations of the unconscious in movement, speech and development. Bethel, Connecticut. Rutledge Books, Inc.: 1997, 119.

250. Freidman, M. Martin Buber: The life of dialogue. 4th ed. London and New York. Routledge. 1955, 98.

251. Sun, R. and Wilson, N. (2014) Roles of implicit processes: instinct, intuition, and personality. Mind Soc (2014) 13: 109–134. DOI 10. 1007/ S11299-0134-4 accessed 07 September 2015 at www.cogsci.rpi.edu/~rsun/ folder-files/sun-personality-jM&S-2014.pdf.

252. Perri, V. Language of the archetype. Explorations of the unconscious in movement, speech and development. Bethel, Connecticut. Rutledge Books, Inc.: 1997, XV.

253. Chamberlain, D.B., 1997. Birth psychology. The fetal senses: A classical view. Accessed 11 April 2013. http://birthpsychology.com/free-article/ fetal-senses-classical-view.

254. Buber, M. I and thou. (Walter Kaufmann, Trans.). New York. Charles Scribner's sons. 1970, 107.

255. Ibid., 107.

256. Buber, M. I and thou. (Walter Kaufmann, Trans.). New York. Charles Scribner's sons. 1970, 89.

257. Sun, R. and Wilson, N. (2014) Roles of implicit processes: instinct, intuition, and personality. Mind Soc (2014) 13: 109–134. DOI 10. 1007/ S11299-0134-4 accessed 07 September 2015 at www.cogsci.rpi.edu/~rsun/ folder-files/sun-personality-jM&S-2014.pdf.

258. Freidman, M. Martin Buber. The life of dialogue. 4th ed. London and New York. Routledge. 1955, 200.

259. Sun, R. and Wilson, N. (2014) Roles of implicit processes: instinct, intuition, and personality. Mind Soc (2014) 13: 109–134. DOI 10. 1007/ S11299-0134-4 accessed 07 September 2015 at www.cogsci.rpi.edu/~rsun/ folder-files/sun-personality-jM&S-2014.pdf.

260. Perri, V. Language of the archetype. Explorations of the unconscious in movement, speech and development. Bethel, Connecticut. Rutledge Books, Inc.: 1997, XV.

261. Bohm, D. Wholeness and the implicate order. Routledge. London and New York. 1980, 140–171.

262. Buber, M. I and thou. (Walter Kaufmann, Trans.). New York. Charles Scribner's sons. 1970, 107, 116.

263. Ibid., 107, 116.

264. Sun, R. and Wilson, N. (2014) Roles of implicit processes: instinct, intuition, and personality. Mind Soc (2014) 13: 109–134. DOI 10. 1007/ S11299-0134-4 accessed 07 September 2015 at www.cogsci.rpi.edu/~rsun/ folder-files/sun-personality-jM&S-2014.pdf.

265. Bohm, D. Wholeness and the implicate order. Routledge. London and New York. 1980, 140–171.

266. Buber, M. I and thou. (Walter Kaufmann, Trans.). New York. Charles Scribner's sons. 1970, 107, 116.

267. Sun, R. and Wilson, N. (2014) Roles of implicit processes: instinct, intuition, and personality. Mind Soc (2014) 13: 109–134. DOI 10. 1007/ S11299-0134-4 accessed 07 September 2015 at www.cogsci.rpi.edu/~rsun/ folder-files/sun-personality-jM&S-2014.pdf.

268. Sun, R. and Wilson, N. (2014) Roles of implicit processes: instinct, intuition, and personality. Mind Soc (2014) 13: 109–134. DOI 10. 1007/ S11299-0134-4 accessed 07 September 2015 at www.cogsci.rpi.edu/~rsun/ folder-files/sun-personality-jM&S-2014.pdf.

269. Buber, M. I and thou. (W. Kaufmann, Trans.). New York. Charles Scribner's sons. 1970, 62, 89.

270. Buber, M. I and thou. (W. Kaufmann, Trans.). New York. Charles Scriber's sons. 1979, 89.

271. Ibid., 89.

272. Sun, R. and Wilson, N. (2014) Roles of implicit processes: instinct, intuition, and personality. Mind Soc (2014) 13: 109–134. DOI 10. 1007/ S11299-0134-4 accessed 07 September 2015 at www.cogsci.rpi.edu/~rsun/ folder-files/sun-personality-jM&S-2014.pdf.

273. Bohm, D. Wholeness and the implicate order. Routledge. London and New York. 1980, 140–171.

274. Sun, R. and Wilson, N. (2014) Roles of implicit processes: instinct, intuition, and personality. Mind Soc (2014) 13: 109–134. DOI 10. 1007/ S11299-0134-4 accessed 07 September 2015 at www.cogsci.rpi.edu/~rsun/ folder-files/sun-personality-jM&S-2014.pdf.

275. Buber, M. I and thou. (W. Kaufmann, Trans.). New York. Charles Scribner's sons. 1970, 89.

276. Ibid., 137.

277. Buber, M. I and thou. (W. Kaufmann, Trans.). New York. Charles Scribner's sons. 1970, 137.

278. Ibid., 89, 58.

279. Buber, M. I and thou. (W. Kaufmann, Trans.). New York. Charles Scribner's sons. 1970, 137.

280. Ibid., 107.

281. Buber, M. I and thou. (W. Kaufmann, Trans.). New York. Charles Scribner's sons. 1970, 107.

282. John 15:5.

283. Buber, M. I and thou. (W. Kaufmann, Trans.). New York. Charles Scribner's sons. 1970, 89.

284. Samuels, A. Jung and the post-Jungians. London and New York. Tavistock/ Routledge. 1985, 58–60.

285. Perri, V. The healing space. Boca Raton. Universal-Publishers. 2014, 52.

286. The Zohar: Pritzker Edition, Volume One. Matt, Daniel C. Stanford. Stanford University Press. 2003.

287. Buber, M. On Judaism. Ed. Nahum N. Glatzer. New York. Schocken Books. 1967, 43.

288. The Zohar: Pritzker Edition, Volume One. Matt, Daniel C. Stanford. Stanford University Press. 2003, LII.

289. The Zohar: Pritzker Edition, Volume One. Matt, Daniel C. Stanford. Stanford University Press. 2003, LII–LIII.

290. Ibid., 2003, LII.

291. Buber, M. I and thou. (W. Kaufmann, Trans.). New York. Charles Scribner's sons. 1970, 89.

292. Ibid., 53–85.

293. Buber, M. I and thou. (W. Kaufmann, Trans.). New York. Charles Scribner's sons. 1970, 107.

294. Ibid., 53–85.

295. Heschel, Abraham J. Moral grandeur and spiritual audacity. Ed. Susannah Heschel. New York. Farrar, Straus, and Giroux. 1996, 384–386.

296. Buber, M. I and thou. (W. Kaufmann, Trans.). New York. Charles Scribner's sons. 1970, 107.

297. Buber, M. On Judaism. Ed. Nahum N. Glatzer. New York. Schocken Books. 1967, 29.

298. Ibid., 29.

299. Buber, M. On Judaism. Ed. Nahum N. Glatzer. New York. Schocken Books. 1967, 29.

300. Ibid., 29.

301. Buber, M. On Judaism. Ed. Nahum N. Glatzer. New York. Schocken Books. 1967, 29.

302. Friedman, M. Martin Buber: The life of dialogue. 4th ed. London and New York. Routledge. 1955, 82.

303. Perri, V. Crowns of thorns. New York, London, Shanghai. Writers Club Press. 2003, 35.

304. Buber, M. I and thou. (W. Kaufmann, Trans.). New York. Charles Scribner's sons. 1970, 89.

305. Matthew 18:20.

306. Samuels, A. Jung and the post-Jungians. London and New York. Tavistock/ Routledge. 1985, 120.

307. Buber, M. I and thou. (W. Kaufmann, Trans.). New York. Charles Scribner's sons. 1970, 116.

308. Buber, M. I and thou. (W. Kaufmann, Trans.). New York. Charles Scribner's sons. 1970, 67.

309. Ibid., 89.

310. Buber, M. I and thou. (W. Kaufmann, Trans.). New York. Charles Scribner's sons. 1970, 116.

311. Ibid., 62.

312. Jung, C.G. The psychology of Kundalini yoga. Ed. Sonu Shamdasani. Princeton. Princeton University Press. Bollingen series xcix. 1996, 74.

313. Ibid., 77.

314. Buber, M. I and thou. (W. Kaufmann, Trans.). New York. Charles Scribner's sons. 1970, 107.

315. Perri, V. Language of the archetype: Explorations of the unconscious in movement, speech, and development. Bethel, Connecticut. Rutledge Books, Inc. 1997, 122–123.

316. Sun, R. and Wilson, N. (2014) Roles of implicit processes: instinct, intuition, and personality. Mind Soc (2014) 13: 109–134. DOI 10. 1007/ S11299-013-0134-4 accessed on line at www.cogsci.rpi.edu/~rsun/folder-files/sun-personality-jM&S-2014.pdf.

317. Buber, M. I and thou. (W. Kaufmann, Trans.). New York. Charles Scribner's sons. 1970, 107.

318. Sun, R. and Wilson, N. (2014) Roles of implicit processes: instinct, intuition, and personality. Mind Soc (2014) 13: 109–134. DOI 10. 1007/S11299-013-0134-4 accessed on line at www.cogsci.rpi.edu/~rsun/folder-files/sun-personality-jM&S-2014.pdf.

319. Buber, M. I and thou. (W. Kaufmann, Trans.). New York. Charles Scribner's sons. 1970, 116.

320. Perri, V. The healing space: Understanding the true nature of inner healing. Boca Raton. Universal-Publishers. 2014.

321. Friedman, M. Martin Buber: The life of dialogue. 4th ed. London and New York. Routledge. 1955, 98–99.

322. Buber, Martin. I and thou. (W. Kaufmann, Trans.). New York. Charles Scribner's sons. 1970, 89.

323. Ibid., 60–61.

324. Perri, Vincent L. The healing space: Understanding the true nature of inner healing. Boca Raton. Universal-Publishers. 2014, 63–66.

325. Samuels, A. Jung and the post Jungians. London and New York: Tavistock/ Routledge: 1985, 151–152.

326. Buber, M. Martin Buber on Psychology and Psychotherapy: Essays, lectures and dialogue. Ed. Judith Buber Agassi. Syracuse University Press. 1999, 21.

327. Buber, M. I and thou. (W. Kaufmann, Trans.). New York. Charles Scribner's sons. 1970, 62, 116.

328. Heschel, Abraham J. Man is not alone. A philosophy of religion. New York. Farrar, Straus, and Giroux. 1951, 12.

329. Heschel, Abraham J. Moral grandeur and spiritual audacity. Ed. Susannah Heschel. New York. Farrar, Straus and Giroux. 1996, 135.

330. Heschel, Abraham J. Moral grandeur and spiritual audacity. Ed. Susannah Heschel. New York. Farrar, Straus and Giroux. 1996, 120–121.

331. Ibid., 120.

332. Heschel, Abraham J. Moral grandeur and spiritual audacity. Ed. Susannah Heschel. New York. Farrar, Strauss and Giroux. 1996, 135.

333. Buber, M. I and thou. (W. Kaufmann, Trans.). New York. Charles Scribner's sons. 1970, 107.

334. Sun, R. and Wilson, N. (2014) Roles of implicit processes: instinct, intuition, and personality. Mind Soc (2014) 13: 109–134. DOI 10. 1007/S11299-013-0134-4 accessed on line at www.cogsci.rpi.edu/~rsun/folder-files/sun-personality-jM&S-2014.pdf.

335. Buber, M. I and thou. (W. Kaufmann, Trans.). New York. Charles Scribner's sons. 1970.

336. Friedman, M. Martin Buber: The life of dialogue. 4th ed. London and New York. Routledge. 1955, 200.

337. Buber, M. I and thou. (W. Kaufmann, Trans.). New York. Charles Scribner's sons. 1970, 67.

338. Ibid., 89.

339. Matthew 27:45–46.

340. Friedman, M. Martin Buber: The life of dialogue. 4th ed. London and New York. Routledge. 1955, 200.

341. Buber, M. I and thou. (W. Kaufmann, Trans.). New York. Charles Scribner's sons. 1970, 107.

342. Perri, V. Advancing conjugate gaze: Advanced concepts in reflex mind-body therapy. Boca Raton. Universal-Publishers. 2013, 24–26.

343. The Zohar: Pritzker Edition, Volume One. Matt, Daniel C. Stanford. Stanford University Press. 2003, LII–LIII.

344. Luke 17:21.

345. Ezekiel 36:26–27.

346. John 14:16.

347. Buber, M. I and thou. (W. Kaufmann, Trans.). New York. Charles Scribner's sons. 1970, 67.

348. Perri, V. The healing space: Understanding the true nature of inner healing. Boca Raton. Universal-Publishers. 2014, 52.

349. Ibid., 15.

350. Perri, V. The healing space. Understanding the true nature of inner healing. Boca Raton. Universal-Publishers. 2014, 15.

351. Buber, M. I and thou. (W. Kaufmann, Trans.). New York. Charles Scribner's sons. 1970, 67.

352. The Zohar: Pritzker Edition, Volume One. Matt, Daniel C. Stanford. Stanford University Press. 2003, LII–LIII.

353. Heschel, Abraham J. Moral grandeur and spiritual audacity. Ed. Susannah Heschel. New York. Farrar, Straus, and Giroux. 1996, 120.

354. Buber, M. I and thou. (W. Kaufmann, Trans.). New York. Charles Scribner's sons. 1970, 127.

355. Heschel, Abraham J. Moral grandeur and spiritual audacity. Ed. Susannah Heschel. New York. Farrar, Straus, and Giroux. 1996, 120.

356. Ibid., 120.

357. Buber, M. I and thou. (W. Kaufmann, Trans.). New York. Charles Scribner's sons. 1970, 67.

358. Friedman, M. Martin Buber: The life of dialogue. 4th ed. London and New York. Routledge. 1955, 22.

359. Ibid., 23.

360. Heschel, Abraham J. Moral grandeur and spiritual audacity. Ed. Susannah Heschel. New York. Farrar, Straus, Giroux. 1996, 204.

361. Buber, M. I and thou. (W. Kaufmann, Trans.). New York. Charles Scribner's sons. 1970, 116.

362. Heschel, Abraham J. Moral grandeur and spiritual audacity. Ed. Susannah Heschel. New York. Farrar, Straus, Giroux. 1996, 204.

363. Buber, M. I and thou. (W. Kaufmann, Trans.). New York. Charles Scribner's sons. 1970, 107.

364. Friedman, M. Martin Buber: The life of dialogue. 4th ed. London and New York. Routledge. 1955, 98–99.

365. Buber, M. I and thou. (W. Kaufmann, Trans.). New York. Charles Scribner's sons. 1970, 67.

366. Perri, V. The healing space. Understanding the true nature of inner healing. Boca Raton. Universal-Publishers. 2014, 63–66.

367. Buber, Martin. I and Thou. (W. Kaufmann, Trans.) New York. Charles Scribner's sons. 1970, 107.

368. Buber, M. On Judaism. Ed. Nahum N. Glatzer. New York. Schocken Books. 1967, 72.

369. Friedman, M. Martin Buber: The life of dialogue. 4th ed. London and New York. Routledge. 1955, 137.

370. Buber, M. I and thou. (W. Kaufmann, Trans.). New York. Charles Scribner's sons. 1970, 127, 137.

371. Ibid., 89.

372. Perri, V. The healing space: Understanding the true nature of inner healing. Boca Raton. Universal-Publishers. 2014, 63–66.

373. Heschel, Abraham J. Moral grandeur and spiritual audacity. Ed. Susannah Heschel. New York. Farrar, Straus, Giroux. 1966, 204.

374. Buber, M. I and thou. (W. Kaufmann, Trans.). New York. Charles Scribner's sons. 1970, 107.

375. Sun, R. and Wilson, N. (2014) Roles of implicit processes: instinct, intuition, and personality. Mind Soc (2014) 13: 109–134. DOI 10. 1007/S11299-013-0134-4 accessed on-line at www.cogsci.rpi.edu/~rsun/folder-files/sun-personality-jM&S-2014.pdf.

376. Freidman, M. Martin Buber: The life of dialogue. 4th ed. London and New York. Routledge. 1955, 200–201.

377. Buber, M. I and thou. (W. Kaufmann, Trans.). New York. Charles Scribner's sons. 1970, 89.

378. Held, Shai. Abraham Joshua Heschel. The call of transcendence. Bloomington and Indianapolis. Indiana University Press. 2013, 20.

379. Nakajima, Teruo and Ono, Taketoshi, eds. *Emotion, Memory, and Behavior*. Boca Raton, New York, London, Tokyo, 1995, 157.

380. Perri, Language of the archetype. Explorations of the unconscious s in movement, speech, and development. Bethel, CT. Rutledge Books, Inc. 1997, 114.

381. The brain from top to bottom. Accessed on line 01/14/2014 @http://thebrain.mcgill.ca/flash/ii/10/i_10_cr_lan/i10_cr_lan.html.

382. Perri, V. Language of the archetype. Explorations of the unconscious in movement, speech and development. Bethel, Ct. Rutledge Books, Inc. 1997, 114.

383. Chamberlain, D.B., 1997. Birth psychology. The fetal senses: A classical view. Accessed 11 April 2013. http://birthpsychology.com/free-article/fetal-senses-classical-view.

384. Nakajima, Teruo and Ono, Taketoshi, eds. *Emotion, Memory, and Behavior.* Boca Raton, New York, London, Tokyo, 1995, 157.

385. Perri, V. Language of the archetype. Explorations of the unconscious in movement, speech and development. Bethel, Ct. Rutledge Books, Inc. 1997, 114.

386. Buber, M. I and thou. (W. Kaufmann, Trans.). New York. Charles Scribner's sons. 1970, 89.

387. Ibid., 89.

388. Heschel, Abraham J. Moral grandeur and spiritual audacity. Ed. Susannah Heschel. New York. Farrar, Straus and Giroux. 1996, 204.

389. Ibid., 204.

390. Buber, M. I and thou. (W. Kaufmann, Trans.). New York. Charles Scribner's sons. 1970, 89.

391. Heschel, Abraham J. Moral grandeur and spiritual audacity. Ed. Susannah Heschel. New York. Farrar, Straus and Giroux. 1996, 204.

392. Buber, M. I and thou. (W. Kaufmann, Trans.). New York. Charles Scribner's sons. 1970, 89.

393. Heschel, Abraham J. Moral grandeur and spiritual audacity. Ed. Susannah Heschel. New York. Farrar, Straus and Giroux. 1996, 204.

394. Buber, M. I and thou. (W. Kaufmann, Trans.). New York. Charles Scribner's sons. 1970, 107.

395. Heschel, Abraham J. Moral grandeur and spiritual audacity. Ed. Susannah Heschel. New York. Farrar, Straus and Giroux. 1996, 120–121.

396. Buber, M. I and thou. (W. Kaufmann, Trans.). New York. Charles Scribner's sons. 1970, 89.

397. Ibid., 128.

398. Jung, C.G. Psychology and alchemy. 2nd ed. (R.F.C. Hull, Trans.). Princeton. Princeton University Press. Bollingen series XX. 1953, 353.

399. John 14:16.

400. Matthew 26:39.

401. Buber, M. I and thou. (W. Kaufmann, Trans.). New York. Charles Scribner's sons. 1970, 89.

402. Ibid., 89.

403. Mark 9:2–8.

404. Buber, M. I and thou. (W. Kaufmann, Trans.). New York. Charles Scribner's sons. 1970, 89.

405. Ibid., 89.

406. Buber, M. I and thou. (W. Kaufmann, Trans.). New York. Charles Scribner's sons. 1970, 62.

407. Friedman, M. Martin Buber: The life of dialogue. 4th ed. London and New York. Routledge. 1955, 200–201.

408. Jwing-Ming, Yang. The roots of Chinese Qigong: Secrets for health, longevity and enlightenment. Roslindale, Massachusetts: YMAA Publication Center, 1989, 1997, 87.

409. Friedman, M. Martin Buber: The life of dialogue. 4th ed. London and New York. Routledge. 1955, 201.

410. Buber, M. I and thou. (W. Kaufmann, Trans.). New York. Charles Scribner's sons. 1970, 89.

411. Friedman, M. Martin Buber: The life of dialogue. 4th ed. London and New York. Routledge. 1955, 201.

412. Matthew 10:8.

413. Buber, M. I and thou. (W. Kaufmann, Trans.). New York. Charles Scribner's sons. 1970, 62.

414. Matthew 8:26.

415. Matthew 26:39.

416. Matthew 26:39.

417. Matthew 26:39.

418. Buber, M. I and thou. (W. Kaufmann, Trans.). New York. Charles Scribner's sons. 1970, 116.

419. Friedman, M. Martin Buber: The life of dialogue. 4th ed. London and New York. Routledge. 1955, 119.

420. Ibid., 119.

421. Bercholz, S., and Sherab Chodzin Kohn, eds. The Buddha and his teachings. Boston. Shambhala Publications, Inc. 2003, 57.

422. Ibid., 58.

423. Matthew 26:39.

424. Bercholz, S. and Sherab Chodzin Kohn, eds. The Buddha and his teachings. Boston. Shambhala Publications, Inc. 2003, 57–59.

425. Perri, V. Conjugate gaze somato-emotional release: A novel approach to physiotherapeutic mind-body therapy. Universal Publishers. USA. 2014, 81.

426. Friedman, M. Martin Buber: The life of dialogue. 4th ed. London and New York. Routledge. 1955, 96.

427. Perri, V. Conjugate gaze adjustive technique: An introduction to innovative chiropractic theory and practice. Universal Publishers. USA. 2001, 97.

428. Buber, M. I and thou. (Walter Kaufmann, Trans.). New York. Charles Scribner's sons. 1970, 89.

429. Bercholz, S. and Sherab Chodzin Kohn, eds. The Buddha and his teachings. Boston. Shambhala Publications, Inc. 2003, 134–140.

430. Praglin, L. (2006). The Nature of the "In-Between" in D.W. Winnicott's Concept of Transitional Space and in Martin Buber's das Zwischenmenschliche. Universitas, Vol. 2 Issue 2 (Fall 2006) accessed on-line at www.uni.edu/universitas/archive/fall 06/pdf/art_praglin.pdf.

431. John 12:14.

432. Jung, C. G. Psychology and alchemy. (R. F. C. Hull, Trans.). 2nd ed. Princeton. Princeton University Press. Bollingen series xx. 1953, 133.

433. Buber, M. I and thou. (Walter Kaufmann, Trans.). New York. Charles Scribner's sons. 1970, 67.

434. Ibid., 89.

435. Friedman, M. Martin Buber: The life of dialogue. 4th ed. London and New York. Routledge. 1955, 303.

436. Heschel, Abraham J. Moral grandeur and spiritual audacity. Ed. Susannah Heschel. New York. Farrar, Straus and Giroux. 1996, 329.

437. Friedman, M. Martin Buber: The life of dialogue. 4th ed. London and New York. Routledge. 1955, 304.

438. Ibid., 154.

439. Buber, M. I and thou. (Walter Kaufmann, Trans.). New York. Charles Scribner's sons. 1970, 107.

440. Friedman, M. Martin Buber. The life of dialogue. 4th ed. London and New York. Routledge. 1955, 99.

441. Ibid., 355–356.

442. Heschel, Abraham J. Moral grandeur and spiritual audacity. Ed. Susannah Heschel. New York. Farrar, Straus and Giroux. 1996, 308.

443. Ibid., 310.

444. Heschel, Abraham J. Moral grandeur and spiritual audacity. Ed. Susannah Heschel. New York. Farrar, Straus and Giroux. 1996, 163.

445. Ibid., 160.

446. Matthew 19:26.

447. Heschel, Abraham J. Moral grandeur and spiritual audacity. Ed. Susannah Heschel. New York. Farrar, Straus and Giroux. 1996, 321.

448. Ibid., 161.

449. Buber, Martin. I and thou. (Walter Kaufmann, Trans.). New York. Charles Scribner's sons. 1970, 107.

450. The Zohar: Pritzker Edition, Volume One. Matt, Daniel C. Stanford. Stanford University Press. 2003, LII

451. John 8:12.

452. Buber, Martin. I and thou. (Walter Kaufmann, Trans.). New York. Charles Scribner's sons. 1979, 13–85.

453. Ibid., 107.

454. Heschel, Abraham J. Moral grandeur and spiritual audacity. Ed. Susannah Heschel. New York. Farrar, Straus and Giroux. 1996, 161.

455. Buber, Martin. I and thou. (Walter Kaufmann, Trans.). New York. Charles Scribner's sons. 1970, 13–85.

456. Ibid., 58.

457. Heschel, Abraham J. Moral grandeur and spiritual audacity. Ed. Susannah Heschel. New York. Farrar, Straus, and Giroux. 1996, 161.

458. Ibid., 161.

459. Heschel, Abraham J. Moral grandeur and spiritual audacity. Ed. Susannah Heschel. New York. Farrar, Straus, and Giroux. 1996, 161.

460. Friedman, M. Martin Buber: The life of dialogue. 4th ed. London and New York. Routledge. 1955, 200–201.

461. Perri, V. Advancing conjugate gaze: Advanced concepts in reflex mind-body therapy. Universal Publishers. USA. 2013, 47–49.

462. Nakajima, Teruo and Ono, Taketoshi, eds. Emotion, Memory and Behavior. Boca Raton, New York, London, Tokyo, 1995, 157.

463. Nakajima, Teruo and Oto, Taketoshi, eds. Emotion, Memory and Behavior. Boca Raton, New York, London, Tokyo, 1995, 157.

464. Buber, Martin. I and Thou. (Walter Kaufmann, Trans.) New York. Charles Scribner's sons. 1970, 89.

465. Menon, V. (2015). Salience Network. In: Arthur W. Toga, editor. Brain Mapping: An Encyclopedic Reference, vol. 2, pp. 597–611. Academic Press: Elsevier @ http://www.elsevier.com/locate/permissionuse material.

466. Bear, M.F., Conners, B.W. and Paradiso, M.A. Neuroscience. Exploring the Brain. 2nd. Ed., Philadelphia, Pennsylvania: Lippincott Williams and Wilkins, 2001, 657, 826.

467. Buber, Martin. I and Thou. (Walter Kaufmann, Trans.) New York. Charles Scribner's sons. 1970, 89.

468. White, Leonard E. Ph.D. 2018. Circuity of the basal ganglia. Part 3 @https://www.coursera.org/lecture/medical-neuroscience/circuity-of-the-basal-ganglia-part-3-hmsIW.

469. Friedman, M. Martin Buber: The life of dialogue. 4th ed. London and New York. Routledge. 1955, 93.

470. Ibid., 93–94.

471. Friedman, M. Martin Buber: The life of dialogue. 4th ed. London and New York. Routledge. 1955, 93.

472. Singer, T. The neuronal basis and ontogeny of empathy and mind reading: review of literature and implications for future research. Neurosci Rev. 2006; 30(6): 855–63 accessed @ https://www.ncbi.nlm.nih.gov/pmc/articles/PMC 2899886/Saliency, switching, attention and control: a network model of insula function. Vinod Menon and Lucina Q. Uddin.

473. Immordino-Yang MH, McColl A, Damasio H, Damasio A Proc Natl Acad Sci USA. 2009 May 12; 106(19): 8021–6 accessed @ https://www.ncbi.nlm.nih.gov/pmc/articles/PMC 2899886/Saliency, switching, attention and control: a network model of insula function. Vinod Menon and Lucina Q Uddin.

474. Heschel, Abraham J. Moral grandeur and spiritual audacity. Ed. Susannah Heschel. New York. Farrar, Straus and Giroux. 1996, 120.

475. Zohar, Dana. The Quantum Self. New York: Quill/William Morrow, 1990, 79.

476. Ibid., 83.

477. Perri, Vincent. Language of the Archetype: Explorations of the unconscious in movement, speech and development. Bethel, Ct. Rutledge Books, Inc. 1997, 79–81.

478. Ibid., 43.

479. Nakajima, Teruo and Ono, Taketoshi., et al. Emotion, Memory, and Behavior. Boca Raton, New York, London, Tokyo, 1995, 79.

480. Aliana Maren, Craig Harsten and Robert Pap. Handbook of Neural Computing Applications. San Diego, California: Academic Press Inc., 1990, 36.

481. Nakajima, Teruo and Ono, Taketoshi, et al. Emotion, Memory, and Behavior. Boca Raton, New York, London, Tokyo, 1995, 162.

482. Friedman, M. Martin Buber: The life of dialogue. 4th ed. London and New York. Routledge. 1955, 84–97.

483. Buber, Martin. I and Thou. (Walter Kaufmann, trans.). New York. Charles Scribner's sons. 1970, 116.

484. Jung, C.G. Psychology and Alchemy. Princeton: Princeton University Press: Bollingen Series. 1968, 137–138.

485. Friedman, M. Martin Buber: The life of dialogue. 4th ed. London and New York. Routledge. 1955, 84–97.

486. Buber, Martin. I and Thou. (Walter Kaufmann, trans.). New York. Charles Scribner's sons. 1970, 137.

487. Ibid., 53.

488. Buber, Martin. I and Thou. (Walter Kaufmann, trans.). New York. Charles Scribner's sons. 1970, 137.

489. Ibid., 116.

490. Buber, Martin. I and Thou. (Walter Kaufmann, trans.). New York. Charles Scribner's sons. 1970, 67.

491. Friedman, M. Martin Buber: The life of dialogue. 4th ed. London and New York. Routledge. 1955, 224.

492. Ibid., 224.

493. Buber, M. I and Thou. (Walter Kaufmann, trans.). New York. Charles Scribner's sons. 1970, 89.

494. Ibid., 107.

495. Jung, C.G. Psychology and alchemy. Princeton: Princeton University Press: Bollingen Series. 1968, 83.

496. Ibid., 83.

497. Buber, Martin. I and Thou. (Walter Kaufmann, trans.). New York. Charles Scribner's sons. 1979, 116.

498. Held, Shai. Abraham Joshua Heschel.: The call of transcendence. Bloomington and Indianapolis. Indiana University Press. 2013, 4.

499. Buber, Martin. I and Thou. (Walter Kaufmann, trans.). New York. Charles Scribner's sons. 1970, 89.

500. Perri, Vincent. The Healing Space: Understanding the true nature of inner healing. Boca Raton. Universal Publishers. 2014.

501. Held, Shai. Abraham Joshua Heschel: The call of transcendence. Bloomington and Indianapolis. Indiana University Press. 2013, 228.

502. Ibid., 228.

503. Perri, Vincent. Conjugate Gaze Somato-Emotional Release: A novel approach to physiotherapeutic mind-body therapy. USA. Universal Publishers. 2014, 81.

504. Buber, Martin. I and Thou. (Walter Kaufmann, trans.). New York. Charles Scribner's sons. 1970, 89.

505. Friedman, M. Martin Buber: The life of dialogue. 4th ed. London and New York. Routledge. 1955, 200–201.

506. Perri, Vincent. Language of the Archetype. Explorations of the unconscious in movement, speech and development. Bethel, Ct. Rutledge Books, Inc. 1997.

507. Held, Shai. Abraham Joshua Heschel. The call of transcendence. Bloomington and Indianapolis. Indiana University Press. 2013, 228.

508. Ibid., 204.

509. Buber, Martin. I and Thou. (Walter Kaufmann, trans.). New York. Charles Scribner's sons. 1970, 89.

510. Ibid., 89.

511. Buber, Martin. I and Thou. (Walter Kaufmann, trans.). New York. Charles Scribner's sons. 1970, 89.

512. Ibid., 137.

513. Buber, Martin. I and Thou. (Walter Kaufmann, trans.). New York. Charles Scribner's sons. 1970, 137.

514. Friedman, M. Martin Buber: The life of dialogue. 4th ed. London and New York. Routledge. 1955, 224.

515. Buber, Martin. I and Thou. (Walter Kaufmann, trans.). New York. Charles Scribner's sons. 1970.

516. Held, Shai. Abraham Joshua Heschel. The call of transcendence. Bloomington and Indianapolis. Indiana University Press. 2013, 4.

517. Ibid., 4.

518. Held, Shai. Abraham Joshua Heschel. The call of transcendence. Bloomington and Indianapolis. Indiana University Press. 2013, 220.

519. Buber, Martin. I and Thou. (Walter Kaufmann, trans.). New York. Charles Scribner's sons. 1970, 89.

520. Ibid., 89.

521. Held, Shai. Abraham Joshua Heschel. The call of transcendence. Bloomington and Indianapolis. Indiana University Press. 2013, 34.

522. Ibid., 34.

523. Heschel, Abraham Joshua. I Asked For Wonder: A spiritual anthology. New York. The Crossroad Publishing Company. 2014, 20.

524. Matthew 18:3–4.

525. Held, Shai. Abraham Joshua Heschel. The call of transcendence. Bloomington and Indianapolis. Indiana University Press. 2013, 34.

526. Heschel, Abraham Joshua. I Asked For Wonder: A spiritual anthology. New York. The Crossroad Publishing Company. 2014, 20.

527. Ibid., 20.

528. Friedman, M. Martin Buber: The life of dialogue. 4th ed. London and New York. Routledge. 1955, 200.

529. Buber, Martin. I and Thou. (Walter Kaufmann, trans.). New York. Charles Scribner's sons. 1970, 89.

530. Ibid., 89.

531. Heschel, Abraham Joshua. I Asked For Wonder: A spiritual anthology. New York. The Crossroad Publishing Company. 2014, 119.

532. Ibid., 20.

533. Heschel, Abraham Joshua. Moral Grandeur and Spiritual Audacity. Ed. Susannah Heschel. New York. Farrar, Straus and Giroux. 1996, 163.

534. Buber, Martin. I and Thou. (Walter Kaufmann, trans.). New York. Charles Scribner's sons. 1970, 67.

535. Buber, M. Martin Buber on Psychology and Psychotherapy: Essays, lectures, and dialogue. Ed. Judith Buber Agassi. Syracuse University Press. 1999.

536. Buber, Martin. I and Thou. (Walter Kaufmann, trans.). New York. Charles Scribner's sons. 1970, 89.

537. Ibid., 21.

538. Friedman, M. Martin Buber: The life of dialogue. 4th ed. London and New York. Routledge. 1995, 200–201.

539. Samuels, Andrew. Jung and the post-Jungians. London and New York. Tavistock/Routledge. 1985, 58–60.

540. Friedman, M. Martin Buber: The life of dialogue. 4th ed. London and New York. Routledge. 1955, 93–94.

541. Ibid., 93–94.

542. Heschel, Abraham Joshua. Moral Grandeur and Spiritual Audacity. Ed. Susannah Heschel. New York. Farrar, Straus, and Giroux. 1996, 204, 293.

543. Buber, M. Martin Buber on Psychology and Psychotherapy: Essays, lectures, and dialogue. Ed. Judith Buber Agassi. Syracuse University Press. 1999, 3–16.

544. Friedman, M. Martin Buber: The life of dialogue. 4th ed. London and New York. Routledge. 1955, 96–97.

545. Ibid., 97.

546. Friedman, M. Martin Buber: The life of dialogue. 4th ed. London and New York. Routledge. 1955, 97.

547. Ibid., 96.

548. Buber, Martin. I and Thou. (Walter Kaufmann, trans.) New York. Charles Scribner's sons. 1970, 89.

549. Ibid., 67.

550. Friedman, M. Martin Buber: The life of dialogue. 4th ed. London and New York. Routledge. 1955, 65.

551. Ibid., 65.

552. Friedman, M. Martin Buber. The life of dialogue. 4th ed. London and New York. Routledge. 1955, 65.

553. Buber, M. Martin Buber on Psychology and Psychotherapy: Essays, lectures, and dialogue. Ed. Judith Buber Agassi. Syracuse University Press. 1999, 63.